D1033927

WITHDRAWN

Hutchins Library
of
Berea College

Berea, Kentucky

WANTING

ONLY

TO BE

HEARD

WANTING

ONLY

TO BE

HEARD

JACK DRISCOLL

The University of Massachusetts Press

Amherst

This book is the winner of the Associated Writing Programs 1991 Award in Short Fiction. AWP is a national, nonprofit organization dedicated to serving American letters, writers, and programs of writing. AWP's headquarters are at Old Dominion University, Norfolk, Virginia.

Copyright © 1992 by Jack Driscoll
All rights reserved
Printed in the United States of America
LC 92-5109
ISBN 0-87023-808-6
Designed by Kristina E. Kachele
Set in Aster with Galliard Display
Printed and bound by Thomson-Shore, Inc.

Library of Congress Cataloging-in-Publication Data
Driscoll, Jack, 1946–
Wanting only to be heard / Jack Driscoll.
p. cm.
ISBN 0–87023–808–6 (alk. paper)
I. Title.
PS3554.R496W36 1992
813'.54—dc20   *92–5109*
                          CIP

British Library Cataloguing in Publication data are available.

D7823W

DRISCOLL, JACK, 1946-

WANTING ONLY TO BE HEARD

IN MEMORY OF MY FATHER,
John Francis Driscoll
(1913–1988)

. . . it is failure that makes a man enter into himself and reckon up his resources. And though he had made up his mind to retire from the world in hermit fashion, yet he was irrationally moved by this sense of loneliness which had come to him in the hour of renunciation. It hurt him. Nothing is more painful than the shock of sharp contradictions that lacerate our intelligence and our feelings.

JOSEPH CONRAD,
Victory

ACKNOWLEDGMENTS

These stories, sometimes in a slightly different form, appeared in the following publications:
Black Ice, no. 4 (1988): "Flea to Jesus"; *Denver Quarterly* 27, no. 2 (1992): "Payment"; *Epoch* 40, no. 3 (1991): "The Season of Families"; *Georgia Review* 41, no. 4 (Winter 1987): "Wanting Only to Be Heard," and 45, no. 4 (Winter 1992): "Devotion"; *Gettysburg Review* (Spring 1991): "Bud and Goliath in the Batting Cage"; *Missouri Review* 10, no. 1 (1987): "Death Parts"; *New Virginia Review* 8 (Fall 1991): "Wish Pennies"; *Ohio Review,* no. 37 (1986): "Miss Dunn"; *Pennsylvania Review* 1, no. 2 (Fall 1985): "Pig and Lobsters"; *Ploughshares* 16 (1991): "Killing Time"; *Quarterly West,* no. 31 (Summer-Fall 1990): "The Wilderness State"; *Southern Review* (Spring 1991): "From Here to There"; *West Branch* 27 (Fall 1990): "Fugitive"; *Western Humanities Review* 45, no. 2 (1991): "August Sales"; *Witness* 4, no. 1 (1990): "The Tryout," and 5, no. 1 (1992): "Land Tides."

A group of these stories won the 1988 PEN/Nelson Algren Fiction Award. "The Wilderness State," "Pig and Lobsters," "Miss Dunn," and "The Tryout" were selected for the PEN Syndicated Fiction Project.

My thanks to Terry Caszatt, who encouraged me in the early going, and to Noel Schroeder, who showed me the woods.

CONTENTS

PART 1

Wanting Only to Be Heard

Ashelby Judge was an odd name for a kid growing up in northern Michigan, so we just called him by his last name, Judge. Everyone did. In a way he always was holding court, pronouncing sentence: Kevin Moriarty was a first-class cockroach, Jake Reardon a homo from the word "go." He had once called me a dicksqueeze, but later he took it back, gladly, he said, having indicted me prematurely. I was okay, he said, I really was, that being the final verdict.

Judge was not easy sometimes, but I liked him. I liked his impatience with boredom and the way he gathered all the pertinent information in the end, the evidence to prove or discredit a story. He always proceeded step-by-step, building an airtight case for whatever he was defending or attacking, whatever he was attempting to pin down. It wouldn't have surprised me, forty years later, to read he'd been appointed to the Supreme Court. Judge Ashelby Judge. Or, for the sake of a joke, Judge Judge. I liked famous names that repeated or almost did, names like Robin Roberts or Ricky Ricardo, or even slant combos like Jack Johnson. The duplication had a friendly ring, a sense of conviction and rectitude, the feeling that they really knew who they were and liked it and would never entirely grow up, grow old.

It was a Friday night, no wind for a change, and we were fishing smelt, three of us inside my father's shanty, when Judge told me and Timmy Murphy about the claustrophobic Irish setter who, after being locked all afternoon in a fishing hut on Torch Lake, jumped right through the spearing hole just after dark and, ten or twelve feet under the ice, swam toward the faint, opalescent glow of another shanty almost fifty yards away (someone later measured it) and came bursting up there from the muck like some monster awakened, the water swelling, convulsing up over the wooden floor. That one simile, "like some monster," was the only embellishment, Judge's single artistic touch.

He was not a natural storyteller who tested his listeners by saying, "imagine this," or "pretend that," or "just think if," and on and on, suspending their willingness to imprint the local tales into myth. He despised the "what then, what next" demands made on every story. Which was exactly what Timmy was doing, all excited and ahead of himself as usual: "What'd the guy do? Holy shit, I bet he croaked right there. I can't believe it, a dog under the ice. That's great!" Judge, calculatedly slow and flat, said the guy was plenty scared, who wouldn't be, but not berserk scared the way you might expect. He was old, Judge said—a simple observation of fact, like what day it was or how cold. He never speculated that age buffered the body's reaction to shock or trauma, but I translated it that way anyhow, without thinking. "Who cares?" Timmy asked. "Twenty, fifty-seven, a hundred-and-two years old. It doesn't matter." But it did, the way it mattered that the dog was an Irish setter and male and was abandoned by his owner who loved him but hadn't gotten any fish, and instead of a quick trip to the 7-Eleven for a six-pack of Stroh's, he drank away the afternoon, alone in a bar that said just that in red neon, *BAR*, just outside Bellaire, forgetting the dog, and playing, over and over on the free juke box, Patsy Cline's "Walking after Midnight." Which was about the time he left the bar, broke and drunk, and halfway home remembered the dog and right there, on 137, opened his window full for the few seconds it took him to slow down and power slide into the other lane, the pickup fishtailing back up the gradual incline beneath the stars, the hook of the moon. And it mattered that he honked his horn a couple of times from the lake's edge, his shanty invisible somewhere beyond the white perimeter of his high beams. That was the real story, that sadness, and the way the guy, on both knees, fiddled with the combination lock until his fingers went numb, the whole time talking to the dog who wasn't even there. When he finally opened the door and lit the lantern, the white flame hissing in the mantle, he stepped back outside and screamed the dog's name a single time across the emptiness.

Judge said you could measure a story by its private disclosures, by how far a person came forward to confess a part of himself, asking forgiveness. The dramatics meant nothing, those exaggerations that served only to engage our obvious and temporary fascinations. And he continued, refining the art of meticulous detachment from such a rare and bizarre event, saying he didn't care what the Irish setter looked like emerging—a giant muskie or sturgeon or a red fresh-water seal. "The fact is," he repeated, "it was a hundred-pound dog. That's it, cut and dried!" I thought maybe the "cut and dried" part was a pun, and I smiled until Timmy, really miffed, said, "You take away all the magic. You make everything too real, too damn ordinary." But Timmy was at least partly wrong. There *was* something principled about facts, something stark and real that required nothing but themselves to survive. Maybe that's why I liked "Dragnet" so much, the claim that it was a true story, that the sentence handed down after the last TV commercial was really being served. I thought of that while leaving the shanty to pee and to check the tip-ups set for browns behind us in the dark. My father let me and my buddies use the shanty on week nights while he worked at the Fisk. Usually he'd drop us off at the state park and we'd take turns dragging the sled with the minnow bucket and spud and the gallon can of stove gas straight toward the village of fifty or sixty tiny structures in a cluster set over the deep water. It was easy to find my father's shanty because it was separated a little ways from the others, and because of the spoked hubcap from a Cadillac Eldorado he'd nailed to the door. His house sign, he called it. Other guys had other things, and it was fun to traipse around at night out there, just looking around, the world glaciated, frozen so tight you could feel your breath clinging to the fine hairs on your face. The name of each owner and town he was from was painted on every shanty—that was the law—some from as far south as Clare, though those were the ones that were not used very much. Sometimes as you passed you could hear talking from inside, or good laughter, or country music on the radio, and when you returned to the heat of your own hut, maybe you'd be humming a certain song, surprised by how happy you were, how peaceful, knowing that you belonged. I figured that was why my father decided to fish again after all these years, why he spent most of every weekend out here, calm and without worries.

That wasn't the feeling, however, when I stepped back inside and Judge and Timmy were both just staring into the rectangular hole, staring at the blue rubber-band bobbers and saying nothing. The smelt pail was still empty and half the minnows in the other bucket had turned belly up. My father would have said no big deal, that smelt would go for the dead bait just as good if they were feeding, but either Judge or Timmy, having already given up, had entered a big 0, a goose egg, in the calendar square for February 12th. On good nights you loaded up fast, constant action, and on the homemade speed reels you could bring in two or three smelt at a time, every few minutes without a break. Just three nights earlier my father had recorded 268, and that was by himself. That's how it happened, streaky and unpredictable, and you simply had to like being out there, maybe sharing a Pall Mall around or talking girls if that's what mystery happened to be biting. But on this night of the Irish setter story, everything had gone closemouthed.

"No flags," I said, latching the door and hanging the gaff on a hook above the stove. This was Judge's first time ice fishing, and I knew he was bored—knew it even better when he said to Timmy, "Why not?" responding to whether a person (forget the dog) could survive the 33° water long enough to swim from this shanty to the one closest by, the one that said M. KULANDA, KALKASKA, MI, the largest one on the ice. I'd never seen anybody there, not once.

"Houdini stayed under twenty minutes," Judge said, "under the Detroit River. No wetsuit. Nothing but a pair of pants."

"What was he doing there? A trick?" Timmy asked.

"An escape," Judge corrected, and although Timmy argued, "Trick, escape, whatever he did . . . ," I understood the difference, the dangerous mishandling of a single word so that a story softened, collapsed like a fragile set of lungs.

"Houdini said later he sucked the air pockets, bubbles trapped between the water and ice, and with the current, followed his dead mother's voice until he emerged, a quarter mile downriver." Judge was still staring into the thick, dark water while he talked, until Timmy, excited, just like at first with the Irish setter story, said, "You're shitting me!" Judge, looking up finally, straight-faced and serious, said, "I shit you not," as if under oath, and they both went silent as if the naked truth of Houdini and the Irish setter were tempting them to find out.

It started simple as that, and next thing I knew we were pacing off the distance between the shanties. About thirty yards. I had once stayed underwater in the bathtub for as long as I could, just sliding back holding my nose. I counted a minute and forty-four seconds, long seconds—one, one thousand, two, one thousand, three, the facecloth kind of floating back and forth across my stomach. And sneaking into the Camp Ketch-A-Tonk swimgrounds one night last summer, I breast stroked real close to the sandy bottom, from the Great Raft all the way up to shore. My father did it too, swimming behind me, and without coming up for air he turned and swam halfway back. I was scared, the way you get when someone's been down a long time, maybe just monkeying around, but scaring you just the same. I remembered whispering, "Come up, please come up," and he did, beyond the blue lifeline, gracefully rolling onto his back in a single motion and kicking, eyes closed I imagined, straight out toward whatever secret had surfaced in his memory. That's how it is with the mind, always buoyant, bobbing up and down on that complex sea of recollection.

Judge knocked on Kulanda's door, but nobody was there. "Nobody has been," Timmy said, trying to take charge. "Look around. No footprints anywhere." And I noticed there were no bloodstains from trout or pike tossed into the snow, no frozen minnows. Nothing. The shanty was unlocked, a lousy idea my father always lectured, every time he'd see a door blown open, slapping backwards hard against its hinges. He said that only invited trouble, people snooping around, poking their heads in where they didn't belong, which was exactly what we were doing and I didn't like it and said, "Come on you guys, let's go. Let's get out of here." But when Timmy stepped inside with the lantern, the hut was nearly empty, unused, the kind that just got left sitting there until the ice softened toward spring, and one morning it would be gone forever. Who knows, maybe the owner died or got sick or one Sunday started watching the Pistons on TV with his son-in-law and thought, "Screw the fishing," and that was that for the whole season.

Timmy said, "The guy's got a couch in here," and when he sat down he was staring at a calendar hanging on the opposite wall. It was the kind of calendar I first saw in a gas station in Germfask when my father's station wagon broke down. We were there a good part of the afternoon while the garage owner phoned around until he finally located a water pump at a junkyard in Greighton. The owner's kid drove over to pick it up, and while our fathers small talked engines and horsepower and cubic inches, I snuck into the men's room three or four times to examine, close-up, this woman who was showing me everything, her lips parted just enough to show the pink edge of her tongue. The last time I stepped out my father was waiting by the door and he told me, "Pee out back. I don't want you in there anymore." And that was the feeling I had again in Kulanda's abandoned shanty, of wanting to be there and not, both at the same time. Timmy lowered the lantern to the ice, right under the calendar where the fishing hole should have been, really lighting up the glossy nude, and he said, acting the big shot for this lucky find, "I'd swim anywhere if I could surface between legs like that!"

But it was Judge who decided to really do it, and when my father dropped us off again the next night, we brought, along with the fishing gear, a book on Houdini and a *National Geographic* that showed people in swimsuits running toward the Atlantic Ocean from a snowy beach, in Rhode Island, I think. And Judge talked on and on about some Mr. Maslowski who chopped a large round hole in the ice of his man-made pond, and letting the same red towel drop behind him, he'd hold his hands flat to the sides of his thighs, and each morning, without hesitation, he'd step right through over his head. "For his rheumatism," Judge said. "He worshiped what he called 'certitude,' the ancient and natural cure taking place under the world." Judge had done his homework, covering the Polar Bear Club and U.S. Navy ice divers, the whole time spouting off dates and temperatures and distances, building his case until I believed there was hardly any danger after the initial shock of entering, and he said, staring at me, "You'll be my key witness." And to Timmy, "Who knows what you'll see."

Of course we wanted to see everything: the entry, the look of his eyes behind the mask the instant he surfaced in Kulanda's shanty. But most of all we wanted desperately to watch him moving under the ice, so later that week Judge waterproofed a flashlight with candle wax and electrician's tape, and tested it by lowering the light about twenty feet under the ice. Then Timmy turned off the Coleman lantern and we just stared, all three of us in complete darkness, at that dim glimmer wavering back and forth below us, slow motion, soporific. Judge was the first to speak, his unquestionable right now, presiding and authoritative, factitious as always, but Timmy was making no objections anymore. Judge said, "It works," and we just nodded, accomplices who had learned to listen closely, to rehearse every detail at night in our dreams. "We'll fasten the light to my back," Judge said, "and you guys can walk right above me."

Although we didn't actually fish anymore that week, we'd make up numbers and jot them down each night on my father's calendar, keeping the records current: 114, 226, and— a slow night, Timmy's entry—27. "Just to keep things honest," he said, and we laughed, sitting and clowning around and smoking Pall Malls in what now seemed more like a fort, a refuge—not from the gusting wind, but from the predictable, ordinary things we might have done late after school, like playing Ping-Pong in Timmy's basement, or being home alone tinkering with science projects, or making up a story for English—something sensational and dangerous and totally unbelievable. And whenever my father asked about the fishing I'd tell him Judge and Timmy were splitting up the smelt, taking them home. "Good," he said, as though it were the proper courtesy, the way to make and keep good friends.

If Judge had moments of panic, he never let on, not even on the night of his dive, the Saturday my father decided to work OT. He dropped us at the state park as usual and asked, "You got a ride back?"—and Timmy said, "Yep, my father's picking us up," which was true, but he was coming later than usual. He wouldn't be here until eleven. I don't know why we

wanted the extra time, I really don't. Maybe to change our
minds, or to deny, as Judge would have been the first to point
out, that redemption had anything to do with danger, with
the spectacular moments in a life. But that didn't happen. We
felt transformed, faithful to the careful preparation of an
entire week, and when we started across the ice toward the
village, we believed those two shanties were ours, and ours to
swim between if we wanted, the way you might swim deep
under a cliff in order to come up in a secret cave. After the
first time, it would be easy. And we felt all set, having already
stashed an extra heater and lantern, an army blanket, and
towels in Kulanda's, and we'd hung a thermometer on the
same nail that held what Judge was calling Timmy's porno
queen, but I'd seen him peeking from the couch at those hard
nipples, too, or at the red mercury rising slowly between her
breasts after we'd fired the heater up. Right now chips of ice
were bouncing off her paper flesh as Timmy started to spud
the hole, Judge's exit, and Judge and I left him there and
headed for the other hut. But Judge stopped halfway and
said, "No hurry," and we stood there, watching the lights of
houses blink on the far side of the lake. I felt calm as the lights
vanished and appeared again, floating, I thought, behind a
cold vapor of darkness. And I could hear Timmy in Kulanda's
shanty, a strange thud, thud, as though coming from a great
distance, and already we'd begun walking even farther away.

By the time Timmy got to my father's hut he was breathing
heavily, but he laughed real hard at Judge just sitting there in
his white boxers, the flashlight already taped to his back like
a dorsal fin. "All you need now are scales," Timmy said,
taking off his gloves and coat, and Judge, reaching into his
knapsack, said, "This will have to do," and pulled out a tub of
ball-bearing grease and said, "Cover me real good," scooping
the first brown gob himself with his fingers and sculpting it
up and down one arm. Then he stood there, arms out, and me
and Timmy did the rest, each a skinny side, and Judge, still
joking around said, "Save a little for my dick," and Timmy
said, "A little is all you'll need," as I knelt and reached my

greasy hand into the freezing water to see if this translucent coating really helped, and for that second I was terrified of falling in, the rectangular hole seeming so much like a grave, calm and so carefully ladled out. And without them seeing me, I crossed myself, as my father had taught me to do every, every time before entering strange water.

When I stood up, Timmy, having taken charge of things in Kulanda's shanty, had left again, and Judge was wiping his hands clean on a rag. Then he knotted the white clothesline around his waist—knotted it a couple of times, nothing fancy, but I knew by the way he tugged it wasn't coming free. Still, I wanted something thicker, stronger, a new length of rope, a boat line maybe. Judge said he just needed something to follow back if he got lost or in trouble. It didn't need to be strong. The other end was already tied off around the single roof brace, the rest of the clothesline coiled in wide loops on the floor. Nobody needed to be there to watch or feed it out. It would uncoil smoothly, trailing behind him, a long umbilical cord. Judge, the literalist, would have hated the metaphor, as he would have hated me telling him he looked a little like the creature in *The Creature from the Black Lagoon*, standing there. But he did, primordial and weedy-green in the bright light of the lantern, breathing hard now, hyperventilating for whatever extra oxygen he could squeeze into his lungs. I thought there would be some talk, a final go-over of the details, maybe even a last-minute pardon from this craziness if my father would unexpectedly burst in. But it was Timmy, back again and out of breath, who said, "All set," and Judge simply reached back without hesitation, snapped on the flashlight, then pushed the mask with both hands to his face for better suction and stepped under. I wasn't even sure it happened—he disappeared that fast, without a single word or even a human splash, as though all that body grease had dissolved his bones, his skull, the entire weight of him so that only a ghost drifted under the ice, a vague iridescence.

When we got outside Judge was moving in the right direction. All winter the winds had blown the snow from the ice, so we could see the blurry light down there, and Timmy had one of his own which he kept blinking on and off to let Judge know we were there, right above him, ready to guide him home. The moon was up too, and suddenly the distance to Kulanda's shanty did not seem so far, not with Judge already halfway there and Timmy, all wound up and hooting, "He's got it made, he's got it now!" It was right then Judge's light conked out, and we both stopped, as if Judge would surface there. Neither of us wanted to move, afraid, I think, that we would step on him in the dark and send him deeper, and when we started running for Kulanda's, I circled wide, way behind where Judge would be, hoping he wouldn't hear the slapping panic of our boots, the fear inside us struggling desperately to break free.

Timmy pumped and pumped the lantern until I thought the glass globe would explode. Then he held it just inches above the black water, and he seemed to be staring at the nude, staring all the way through her as if counting each vertebra, the soft curves of her back, and I knew Judge was not coming up. I didn't have to tell Timmy to stay. He was crying now. He was all done, and I think if Judge had surfaced right then, Timmy would have just dropped the lantern and walked away and would never have spoken of this again.

I slipped and fell hard, almost knocking myself out, and in that moment of dizziness, face down on the ice, I imagined Judge staring back, just ten inches away, his black hair wavering in moonlight, his eyes wide-open behind his mask. And I imagined him pointing and pointing and I got up and ran, sweating now, into my father's shanty. I believed the rope twitched or pulsed when I picked it up, something like a nibble, but when I yanked back there was nothing there, just the loose arc of slack, and I remembered my father always shouting from the stern of the boat, "Reel hard, keep reeling," when I thought I'd lost a big one, and this time the weight was there, solid and unforgiving. It was the same heavy feeling of a snag that begins to move just when you're sure it will bust your line, and I knew that bulk dragged backwards was enough to snap any line with a nick or fray, and to hurry was to lose it all. I kept it coming, hand over hand, Judge's body drifting sideways, then back again, always rising slowly from the deep water. I shouted for Timmy four or five times, tilting my head backwards and toward the door, but he did not come. And it was during one of those shouts that the flashlight on Judge's back appeared in the center of the hole, then the whole back hunched in a deadman's float. I could not get him up, my arms weak and shaking, and I hauled back one last time and dropped the rope and grabbed, all in the same motion, his thick hair with both my hands, his face finally lifting out of the water.

His mask was gone and I just held him like that for a long time, one arm under his chin, the lantern dimming. I was stretched on my belly, our cheeks touching, and I had never felt anything so cold, so silent. I knew mouth-to-mouth resuscitation would do Judge no good in this position, his lungs full of water, so maybe I was really kissing him, not trying to reclaim a heartbeat, but to confess, as Judge said, a part of myself, and to ask forgiveness. I did not know how long I could hold him there, though I promised over and over I would never let him slide back to that bottom, alone among those tentacles of weeds. I closed my eyes, and in what must have been a kind of shock or sleep, I drifted into a strange current of emptiness, a white vaporous light, the absolute and lovely beginning of nothing.

I did not see the two ice fishermen hoist Judge from the hole, and I did not remember being carried to Kulanda's shanty or being wrapped in the army blanket on the couch. I awakened alone there, still dizzy but very warm. I was wearing Judge's sweatshirt, the one we had waiting for him when he came up. I did not take it off or even move very much, and I could hear my father's voice just outside the door, though it sounded distant, too, and dull, the blunt echo of a voice approaching. I thought, if he entered, the flood of his words would drown me for good. But only silence followed him in. I did not look up and I did not cry when he touched my head, or when he turned away to face the wall. There would be no sermonizing, no interrogation from him or from anyone else. Not that night anyway. And I noticed, eye-level across from me, that the nude was gone, removed like evidence we didn't want found. The cigarette butts on the floor had disappeared too. And it sounded strange to hear someone knock on the door. My father did not say, "Come in," but a man did, an ambulance driver, and he bent down on one knee and said, "How do you feel now?" I didn't know, but I said, "Good," and I wanted more than anything in the world for the three of us just to stay there, maybe all night, making sure the hole did not freeze over.

Next morning, as we walked together toward the shanties, my father said, "Tell them everything exactly like it happened. There's only one story." What he meant was that the options narrowed and narrowed when the ending was already known.

"They won't keep us long," my father said. "We'll get back home." I thought he might add, "For the Pistons-Celtics game," but he didn't.

It was Sunday morning and sunny, and up ahead, off to the left, I saw a red flag go up from the ice, then someone running toward the tip-up, shaking his gloves off. I watched him set the hook, and after a few seconds, with his left hand, move the gaff a little bit away from the hole. "Probably a pike," my father said, and I was glad he did, so natural, without the conviction of disguise.

There were not all that many people gathered at the shanties, not the way I thought it would be with a lot of photographers and sheriff's department deputies. Timmy was already there. I could see his green hat and his arms flailing like an exhausted swimmer, and for that split second I imagined he was yelling, "Help, help me," and I started to run, not toward him, but the other way, back toward the car. My father caught me from behind, caught me first by the collar, then wrapped both his arms around me and turned me back slowly to face Timmy and whatever version he was carving of the story. My father just held me there and released the pressure gradually and then, after a couple minutes, let me go.

His shanty had been moved back and two divers were adjusting their masks at the side of the hole. I did not know what they were searching for, what more they could possibly find. But they jumped through, one after the other as Judge had, but with black wetsuits and yellow tanks and searchlights sealed with more than candle wax and electrician's tape. The sheriff met us and shook my hand and my father's hand and said Judge's parents were not there and wouldn't be. Then he said, "We've called Marv Kulanda," as though he knew him personally. "He's on his way."

I was okay after that. They kept me and Timmy separated, though we caught each other's eye a couple times. The two fishermen who pulled Judge out kept nodding a lot, and once they pointed at me, both of them did, then shrugged, and they finally left, to fish and talk, I guess, since they walked that way into the village of shanties. I knew the stories wouldn't be the same, but not the same in a way that didn't matter to the law.

The sheriff asked me about approximate times: how long before Timmy ran for help, how long I held Judge partially out of the water—all questions I couldn't answer, and that seemed to be all right. But before he let me go he said, "Whose idea was this?" It was the first time he spoke without detachment, accusatory now, and I did not deny that it was me, though it wasn't, my father the whole time shaking his head, shaking it back and forth, no, no, insisting that could never be.

Before the first diver was helped out of the hole, he tossed Judge's mask a few feet onto the ice, and then, behind it— crumpled into a pulpy ball—what I knew was the calendar nude. I didn't know why that frightened me so much, except that it was a detail I had consciously left out, perhaps to protect Timmy's secret need to destroy the crime of her nakedness, one of the reasons we stayed there and smoked cigarettes and talked big in front of her, already outlining the plans of our story. When the sheriff unwadded the nude she fell apart, and he just shook the wet pieces from his hands. In his investigation for details, she meant nothing—a piece of newspaper, a bag, anything that might have floated by.

We left and my father said, "It's over," and I knew he'd protect me from whatever came next. Behind us I could hear them nailing my father's shanty closed, and I could see, angling beyond us from the shore, a single man, half stepping and half sliding across the ice. I knew that it was Kulanda, who should have locked his hut, who was wishing at that very moment that we had broken in. And beyond him, running between the avenues of shanties, a single dog, tall and thin and red like an Irish setter. But maybe not. Maybe he was something else, barking like that, wanting only to be heard.

PIG AND LOBSTERS

The only book I ever saw my father read was *Fear Strikes Out,* the autobiography of Jimmy Piersall. Even cooking breakfast my father held it open with one hand as though he were a teacher or a priest, his free hand turning down the blue flame flattening under a skillet of home fries on the back burner of the range. Sometimes, slamming the book face down on the table, he would stalk to the kitchen window, enraged, glancing back over one shoulder like a batter heading toward the dugout after arguing a strike three call. "The game ruined him," my father snapped. "Sent him straight to the asylum."

Maybe that's the reason we turned to other things, the reason my father began to stay inside and browse through fat catalogs from Sears and J.C. Penney, always lifting the pages real slow like they were sample squares of wallpaper. Whenever he came to *Hunting & Fishing* he would stare at the aluminum boats, small horsepower outboards, nets and bait buckets, tackle boxes with fancy folding trays. Then he would drift to the bottom of the page for the corresponding code, H-4, and locate the price across the line of dots, lick his left thumb and move on dreaming through this warehouse of glossy merchandise. When a new Wish Book arrived in the mail, he immediately opened it and ripped out the order forms in back, ripped them in half and then again, those tiny paper clouds disappearing into the wastebasket under the sink.

Only once did he make a purchase, a stopwatch to time the distractions of each day. When he wrote a check the first month the rent was raised, he held the sealed envelope just below his eyes, stared over the straight edge and announced, "Fifty-four seconds." Before long he knew the length of every red light on his route home from work, how long it would take to walk to the IGA on Appleton to cash in his six-pack of empties, how much time it took for the bathtub to fill and drain, for the one-legged chickadee to land on the roof of the feeder after my father scattered his new fistful of sunflower seeds. He said he wished he could press the stop button on the watch the moment he entered sleep, or time the distance of each dream. He had heard dreams lasted only a few seconds, brief sprints through the troublesome unconscious. He did not believe this any more than he believed in the brevity of love. "Takes awhile," he said. "If you can, measure love in decades."

But a few years after my mother died he did fall hard and fast for a woman I never met, whose name I never heard. I saw my father nights stationed by the phone, trancelike, inhaling the smoke from his cigarette, containing it a long time, as if in those moments the world came to him calm and quiet. I think he was listening then to the melody of an inner voice. The first sharp ring would always make him grimace, a shock like a man who sleepwalks only to reach out for the strange pulse of an electric fence. Weekend nights he would leave the house after he thought I was asleep, the headlights of the pickup blinking on only after he hit the main road a quarter mile away.

It was October, cold I remember, a Sunday and we were leaning on the railing of the sow's sty, my father's eyes like scales weighing this pig for slaughter. "Next week," he mumbled. But it didn't happen. Instead he invited a guest for dinner and spent the days fussing inside, vacuuming both sides of the cushions on the couch and chairs, moving a glass figurine of a deer a few inches on the dark field of a table, then back again the next day. All week after school I was afraid she would be there waiting, not a guest, but my new mother invading with her woman's touch.

That Saturday my father did not wake me early, though I heard him downstairs arguing with a man from the bank, here, the man emphasized, on a nonbusiness day. This was the second time, the same conversation: bad money and good, loans and risks, foreclosures, preferred customers. But that morning my father felt rich enough to drive to town and return with three live lobsters in a box of crushed ice. He hefted it to the counter, nodded with exaggeration and boasted, "You're damn right!" Then he opened the top, but the lobsters hardly moved until he lifted them out, claws pegged, tails snapping and snapping as if they might swim backwards from my father's hands, their eyes hard and round as B.B.'s, black and hostile, an ancient vision focusing on this bright and hungry world. He dropped them into a drawer of the refrigerator, a bubbly film enclosing each of their tiny mouths.

By eight that night she had still not arrived. On the stove a huge pot of water boiled, oblong bubbles rolling to the surface like waves. Outside the spotlight high on the barn flooded the ground, and inside on the dinner table the flame from a single white candle wavered above the emptiness of our three white plates. Finally, my father went outside, and an hour later when he started back toward the house, it was not to dine, but rather to watch the sow devour the main course live, those lobsters flown a thousand miles to the

Midwest, an emblem of the distance traveled to offer this invitation of love to his first date in fifteen years. And she had stood him up, and now he had the sow around her neck by a rope, straining with his farmer's bulk, trying to manhandle 600 pounds of live pork up the back stairs. Winded, he hollered, "Throw the lobsters on the floor and get out of the way. Get clear!" I could hear the pig grunting and my father grunting back some primal response, promising perhaps, a feast, the language guttural and frighteningly insane.

In panic I felt a sudden need to fold open a clean, wet towel for the lobsters and place them gently side by side, hard-shelled, tentacles wavering, testing the warm and sudden light as if it were invisible water. Instead, I grabbed the largest lobster and yanked out both wooden pegs, yanked them out like thick slivers, and he came struggling back to life, raising both fists above his head. I half dropped, half slid him across a few feet of dull linoleum into the corner by the sink where he wedged himself as if between two rocks. I reached for the others, and when I spun around, the sow was banging through the open door, heaving forward, her solid body shaking the jambs, her narrow eyes fixed on the spot where I was standing. Terrified, I lobbed both lobsters simultaneously into the air toward the sow, as I might a hunk of meat to a wild dog to keep it away. They landed with a thud, with the unexpected heaviness only something live makes with its impact. And the pig was on them, not biting as much as squashing and sucking them in, shells and all, her front legs spread and braced as if against the shallow tide of an ocean.

I do not remember climbing up, but when the pig attacked the corner under my feet, I realized I was standing on the countertop, my body shielded behind the half-opened cabinet door. I did not see my father angling for a shot with his .22, but looking down I watched the pig go suddenly to her knees, that horrible collapse of the body that means the brain's darkness has swallowed this tiny slug. I felt the whole house shake and thought then of passionate killing, my fa-

ther's phrase for the quick and merciful execution of what we
had raised in the sties and coops of the farm. But he did not
slit her throat as he said you must until after he dragged her
with a long rope tied to the tractor outside to the porch. All
night she stayed there, bleeding, her head between her legs
like a dog asleep, its snout just over the edge of the first step.

The biggest lobster was untouched, but dry and slow to
defend itself with what seemed such little claws. My father
would pick it up only with a glove. He never looked at me the
whole time and just walked slowly outside, and standing a
few feet from the barn, side-armed the lobster as hard as he
could against the unpainted boards. It's that sound that is
still so clear, clearer than the sound of the rifle fired inside the
house or the pig's awful squealing at the sharp pain between
its eyes. All this food and slaughter, and in the other room an
uncorked bottle of wine my father would offer no woman so
savage as to leave him alone.

THE TRYOUT

"Now remember," my father said for the umteenth time, driving me to the tryouts for Nick's Nest Peewees, "to keep your head down, your elbows out."

"I know," I said, but I was nervous.

"And watch the ball," he said, "right into the catcher's mitt."

I tried to do that, but it was my first time in a real batter's box and Curt Athas was throwing smoke, all strikes, and I cut late on every pitch, tentative, afraid that the baseball, red seams appearing to tighten, would break inside under my chin. After I'd swung late on three straight fastballs, the coach, Mr. Hassett, yelled from the bench, "Last pitch, hit and run it out!" and my father, a whisper of secret advice behind the backstop, said, "Square up."

He had taught me, just a year ago in front of the huge barn

doors, how to lay down a perfect bunt. His favorite play was the suicide squeeze, and he'd exaggerate the drama from his stretch by checking the imaginary runner inching down the line from third. Then he'd pitch, real slow ones I could handle. But here at Loweke Field I was being tested, intentionally distracted by the catcher's constant chatter: "No batter here. Big whiff, no batter, no batter," and next to this my father's voice seemed the loneliness of poor strategies, the desire for even a small connection, the sound of good wood, the slump finally broken with a soft, clean bunt. So I eased the bat out from my chest, but the ball two-hopped straight back toward the mound where Curt Athas barehanded it, spun and paused, his hard rubber cleats planted in the thick infield grass, his arm cocked to gun me down three full steps from the bag.

I took the field then, and although I had asked to play second base, Mr. Hassett, without even glancing up from his clipboard, pointed to deep right where, in the bright sun all afternoon, I shaded my eyes with my glove, a new Gil McDougald model my father had bought for me with money from his first paycheck at the Fisk, the tire factory in town. And I remember how there was no action except for memory sorting its different moods. And the image? Uniforms. And a team photo hanging above a championship trophy in Nick's Nest, home of the town's first char-broiled hamburgers. A gold mine.

My picture would not be there among these players, though for years my father would stare and stare each time he stopped in to eat on his way to work the night shift. But during that first practice only the coach knew for sure who would not make the initial cut, so I hustled for the one fly ball hit in my direction, routine despite the sun, because for that day everything still mattered.

Like the chubby arms of one Georgie Lopinski, who flinched, jerked his face away from a hard smash to third, and made the tough play blind on the short hop, and smiled to choruses of "Look what I found!" And he did find it, the white skin of the baseball showing in his web, and he knew for the first time in his life how badly he was needed in that one brief moment of the world.

But just as easily, Georgie faded, and the image was in my father's eyes, staring out at me from the empty bleachers, the only parent there to scout the talent in that miniature ballpark, complete with scoreboard and signs telling the distances down each line. He stayed there until practice was over, the bats and balls having disappeared into the darkness of a duffle bag two guys carried toward the open trunk of Mr. Hassett's new Pontiac. Most of the players were already on their bikes, fanning out in all directions home.

Mr. Hassett was the last one on the diamond, down on one knee, unstrapping the last of the canvas bases. He didn't see my father walking out, wide-shouldered, his week's growth of beard like a man superstitious about shaving until the final game of the series is over. But in this case my father was only tired, and what he had seen during the day had nothing to do with the hours we had spent hitting pepper or playing catch beside the cows in the pasture. Or with the sports page spread out at night on the kitchen table where I oiled the deep pocket of my glove. And always, like a good omen under glass, that autograph of Babe Ruth my father got while passing through the dining car on a train from New York in the 1920s.

Before Mr. Hassett could stand up, my father flipped him the ball, a foul he caught earlier and had not tossed back. Then, without a word, he turned and walked slowly to home plate, stepped into the batter's box with one slow practice swing and, staring Mr. Hassett in the eyes, said, "As hard as you can."

Mr. Hassett had never seen this man before, open stance, weight planted firmly on his back foot, ready to step into whatever pitch entered the white silence of the strike zone. Mr. Hassett shrugged, looked left and right to show he was confused, but smiled a little just the same, smiled until my father pointed at him with the fat head of the bat.

"Play ball!" he shouted, the simple and definitive com-
mand of an umpire, and all of a sudden this was no longer the
peewees, the whole park dwarfed by these two men who, in
less than a minute, were caught in the angry backlash of
childhood, the beginning of their separate lives.

And just like that Mr. Hassett, middle-aged and out of
shape, said, "Hit this, you asshole," and gloveless, he wound
up with the one pitch my father could never hit, high and
tight, the bean ball intended to leave him squirming in the
dirt, the long-distance punch, the final retaliation in a game I
would replay from different angles for the rest of my life,
trying to get the call right.

My father had sharp reflexes, but he did not duck, and Mr.
Hassett, watching the ball ricochet off my father's cheekbone, knew there would be no relief. No one was going to beat
my father that late, with evening coming on and this the only
excuse he needed to charge the mound, knowing he couldn't
be restrained when I was the only player around, afraid and
shouting, "Stop!"

My father did not stop, not for a long time. For weeks he
remained almost silent, explaining only that fists finished an
argument, unjumbled what couldn't be talked out. Sometimes it turned out to be the only way. Then maybe you shook
hands, said something simple like, "That's enough," or "It's
over, it's all done now."

But it hadn't gone anything like that with Mr. Hassett who
wouldn't get up from the pitcher's mound. He seemed only to
be eyeing my father's boots as though expecting to be kicked
in the ribs. And only once did he move, and he did that slowly,
twisting his head a little to spit back over the pitching rubber
onto the grass. My father might have walked away the winner then, a little cocky maybe, and nodding. Instead he stood
for several minutes above Mr. Hassett, straddling and taunt-
ing him with weak backhand finger-slaps to the top of his
head, just grazing the thin brown hair combed over from the
side, exposing the slow failure of baldness. And he kept coax-

ing: "Come on, Coach, anytime. Come on, come on, Coach,"
until he was practically chanting, "Coach, Coach, Coach."
And suddenly all effort to force this further seemed puny and
purposeless. Whatever code had justified the attack was forgotten and, in some crazy, backward way, Mr. Hassett had
won, sitting there composed and alone in the center of a baseball diamond for kids, his puffy face cupped in his hands. My
father knew it, glancing back at him just once while walking
away, rubbing his knuckles, itching for just one more shot to
even things up.

But he was no good beyond the impulse to hit whatever
needed hitting head on. So it frightened me when he con-
cocted a scheme, his mind turning this time against the
whole community: coaches and peewee sponsors like Nick's
Nest and Hope Bakery and Holtcamp Hardware, against the
new floodlights and parents cheering the evenings alive.

My season was over—that's what we both understood, and
I went about the business of roaming the apartment in the
tiresome first days of summer. My father, rushed and frus-
trated, told me, "Hang on. Just hold tight for now," and he'd
head out to the garage where he cleared a work space in back.
With his cutting snips he made an aluminum shade from a
Maxwell House coffee can, a kind of reflector hood for the
droplight, then looped the cord over one of the rafters, inching the bulb downward so it hung just a few feet above an old
folding card table. On it he spread out paintings and draw-
ings of dragons he found in books he checked out from the
public library. Instead of sleeping afternoons after work, he
sketched on cardboard and, when he had the dragon pattern
right, he traced it twice on a sheet of plywood. That night, on
the band saw at the Fisk, he cut out two sides of a dragon's
head breathing fire, identical silhouettes three feet high.

My father had made goose decoys the same way, Blues and
Snows and Canadians. And they worked, staked each October among the cut rows, my father on one knee, half blowing,
half spitting into his goosecall, knowing the geese would
turn, banking against the sharp angles of the field, like de-

coys themselves, shadowy and motionless for the instant it took him to step out of that second row of standing corn and open fire. They never seemed so much frightened as tired, their huge wings laboring suddenly to reverse the descent of their bodies. The killing was always so easy—the magic was calling them in, "Speaking their language," as my father put it. Once they committed, you knew you'd get birds. But I couldn't guess what demon my father intended to lure in and slay with the dragon head, or if it even was a decoy, so necessary sometimes to bring the unsuspecting into range.

One Saturday morning, before I awakened, my father posted the peewee league schedule, all evening games, on the refrigerator before he left. No note, just the boxes of cereal and the jar of Tang and one empty blue-and-white bowl on the kitchen table.

He had underlined the Nick's Nest opener in red and, in the margin, a row of exclamation marks, like tiny bats. Staring at them I ate my Sugar Pops standing up, inventing scores for each game, Nick's Nest always losing by a single run. I was the player who would have made the difference, stealing the key base, punching a single through the hole to the opposite field to score the winning run from second. I wrote stories in my head like this a lot.

Had I made the team, even as a sub, I'd be laying out my uniform right now on my bed. Whatever my number was, I'd remember it my whole life, the way I remembered Pee Wee Reese's and Luis Aparicio's and the Scooter's, Phil Rizzuto. Those were the little guys, the speed, the contact hitters who choked up and fought off the good, low hard ones and got their share of walks and base hits, occasionally stroking one up the alley, legging out a triple with a perfect hook slide. Then they'd raise one hand for time, step outside the baseline and slap the dirt from their pants and straighten their socks, the third base coach always stepping over to pat them on the rear end. It was better than a home run, more intimate than that slow, out-of-shape jog around the bases. Triples: that's the stat I examined most on the backs of baseball cards, and I'd trade the power hitters any day, Mantle and Ted Kluszewski and Duke Snyder, for anyone with a bunch of three-baggers.

Before heading outside I gripped my fists, the right one on top of the left, then vice versa, and in slow motion took a few practice swings into the emptiness of the kitchen. I hated my father for what he did, for what he was doing. I hated the way he existed in the world now, so detached and conspiring, and I imagined him talking to himself in the car driving home or at work at the Fisk among the stacks of tires, and I knew it would be a voice breaking apart, fragments of words, a primitive chant only he understood.

He hardly spoke to me anymore, not in the way I needed, not in the way fathers unraveled the tangle of boredom or despair with a simple pep talk, a promise that it might take a little while to make new friends, but no sweat, because he had solutions. So once again I went downstairs alone, and on the lawn between the house and driveway, I threw a rubber ball hard onto the roof where it skipped once or twice across the red shingles toward the steep peak, then rolled back down, always jumping off at tough angles when it hit the ridge of flashing. But I hauled everything in, diving left and right, each catch reviving the old hopes of being discovered, even in my own backyard where, by myself, little else mattered.

When my father pulled in around noon, exhausted and smelling of chickens and dung, the way he had sometimes after towing the spreader behind the tractor all morning on the farm, he said, "Wake me a little before six," and he was smiling as he started up the stairs, tugging the bill of my Tigers baseball cap low over my eyes.

By 7:00 we were driving and it felt good just to be talking about the weather and the standings in the American League East, and how we should keep right on driving to Tiger Stadium, park the station wagon and sleep right there in lot

B, not far from the ticket window. Or maybe, still awake at
two or three in the morning, I'd sneak inside to one of those
long concrete tunnels that led outside to the stands. I imagined how all of a sudden I'd see millions of stars, but not the
same way I did whenever I'd lie on my back on the garage
roof at home. I knew, above that outfield, the stars would take
on different shapes, or not even shapes but feelings, essences
that might start the mind drifting. I wondered if any player
ever returned at night after a bad game, just to sit there
alone, maybe take a seat way out beyond center, and measure
himself against all that darkness staring back. I'd bet even Al
Kaline, Detroit's new superstar, a .340 hitter in just his second season, had moments of doubt that ranged far beyond
the winning and losing of ball games, beyond even the perfect arc of a ball disappearing deep into the lights.

"It's only human," my father said, as if reading my mind.
But he was talking about something else, something earthly
and immediate that would happen within the hour. We were
heading north into farm country, and I asked, "What's human?" and he said, "Revenge."

It was that simple, in the early evening, passing a faded
pink-and-white trailer house with a rough plywood entrance
attached like an afterthought. There were two wooden ducks
marking the end of the dirt driveway—their bright, green
wings rotated backwards in the wind, like cartoon ducks,
and the man leaning against the door jamb in his undershirt
had already balanced his TV on two sawhorses among the
junk outside, the cord trailing. I didn't know why, but I was
sure, after we passed, that he was going to step out with a
handgun and put a single hole dead center into the brain of
that useless screen. I was hoping my father was not armed,
but if he was, I hoped we were on our way to the county dump
to shoot bottles or rats, or maybe the windows and headlights of abandoned cars at the back edges of so many of these
sandy, deserted fields of northern Michigan.

We turned off onto Renolds. The only place up there was
Paul Cutney's fancy new brick ranch house at the end of the

road. He was a chicken farmer with lots of money, a quiet big man like my father, but quiet for different reasons. He hadn't lost a thing in his life but chickens, about fifteen or twenty a day, natural die-off from the 50,000 hens laying night and day in the three long aluminum Quonset barns behind the house.

Right up until the time we lost the farm and moved into town, we'd stop by Paul Cutney's once a week for jumbos or double-yolkers, the eggs so large you couldn't close the cartons. I liked stopping there and, if Paul Cutney lit up a cigarette and started talking with my father, I'd go over to the place on the conveyor belt where the eggs moved slowly under that special light that let you see inside the shells. I'd watch Paul's oldest boy checking each egg for blood spots. "Can't eat those," he'd say, busting them into a pail by his feet. I asked him why not one time and he said the spots were the brains of baby chickens. "They're smart, chickens are," he said, "and that's what develops first, their brains." He smiled then and rubbed my hair, but I believed him, and I always stayed indoors the morning my father slaughtered our few fall chickens, fryers, nothing that ever laid eggs, though I'd check the loft in the barn sometimes anyway, just in case. Paul Jr., my father said, was just giving me the business. He said watch just one chicken dance headless into the October light and I'd know how bright they were. "Zero bright," he half whispered, bending over, carefully plucking the feathers into grocery sacks before burying the heads, the eyes still half open.

I didn't know, when he said "revenge," if it was for having lost the farm or for my mother's sudden death or revenge on Paul Jr. who didn't mean any harm but filled me with crazy ideas about chicken embryos. Or revenge on Mr. Hassett who should have hit me just a half-dozen hot grounders at second base before relinquishing me to the obscurity of deep right where I shaded my eyes in the sun field for an hour until practice was over, not knowing if I'd be cut first thing the next day, my name scratched from the clipboard. All I knew now for certain was that this new life of the neighborhood, and his night job at the Fisk, had my father confused and unable to move with good balance and foresight toward a permanent truce with the world.

We turned into Paul Cutney's chicken farm and I saw, parked next to the house, his dump truck and, on top of the cab, my father's dragon head painted a luminous green with heavy black curves that looked like large thick scales. Even from a distance the eyes seemed wild and yellow, staring off at impossible angles, and Paul Cutney was standing there shaking his head and twirling the ignition key to the dump truck on a small chain around his little finger.

My father did not get out of the station wagon right off. He simply stopped and reached out the window, and Paul Cutney, without taking a step, dropped the key into my father's palm and said, in his slow, raspy voice, "You're really going through with this." That was all. They had obviously been through the conversation earlier in the day, the whole thing, I imagined, me going with him or not, and Paul, staring up as though checking for rain, said only, "Call if you're in trouble." My father said back to him, "There won't be any call."

Paul opened the passenger door by yanking hard on the handle, and then he hoisted me up onto the torn, dark seat. A clear, cut glass rosary, minus the crucifix, dangled above me from the visor. Like us, Paul Cutney was Catholic, and that seemed to matter in some odd way right then, though I was not sure how. Turning around I could see out the rear window that the bed was half-full of dead, white chickens. There was a lot of pink there, too—the pink of their eyelids, the thin veins at the edge of their beaks, pink crowns, and wattles. They did not seem real anymore, piled back there like that, saved all week from the dump for my father. When we pulled out of the driveway, a blizzard of feathers started blowing everywhere behind us, my father shifting through the gears with real purpose now.

As soon as we came over the hump on Hillside, we saw, not the floodlights exactly, but the soft blending of them into a brilliant haze glowing above the ballpark. It seemed magical, holy even, and I said, staring straight ahead, "Please don't go down there. Don't drive near the ballpark." When he looked over at me, I said, and more gently, "Let's just drive around some more," trying to detour him a little while, maybe maneuver him back to Paul Cutney's, where we could leave the dump truck with its load of dead chickens, and that dragon's head on top of the cab like the skimpy remains of a forgotten parade. I reached over to touch his arm and he said, "Don't," and I knew we were going in. Nothing I could say or do could stop that, so I rolled up my window and locked the door and prayed hard to that broken rosary swinging faster and faster, first as the front tires, and then the rear of the truck, bucked the curbstone, and we lurched in low gear down the slight decline behind the bleachers.

Almost everyone in the top couple of rows stood up to watch us, baffled and laughing, until my father, curving wide and coming in behind first base, yanked on the release lever.

I had never seen such iridescence, all that green and then the white shapes of the players scattering across the infield in front of us, and the white of those perfect foul lines stretching taut into the corners of the park. And just beyond the fence in center, in the bottom of the fifth inning, those red numbers hanging by hooks on the scoreboard.

I added up the runs: Nick's Nest was ahead 10-0, a shutout. I felt dizzy, and when the umpire stepped forward across home plate, I mistook him for a priest, black robed, his arms raised, not for a time-out, but in benediction. I reached for the rosary but the light refracting through the sharp octagonals of cut glass turned suddenly violent, spewing hundreds of tiny images simultaneously through the windshield. At a certain angle the dragon's head filled each glass bead, the orange flames more real now, then disappearing and it was my father's mouth wide open, distorted under the pressure of so much light and confusion. Scared and crying I balled up the rosary in my hands, balled and turned it over and over as though I were feeling for its invisible seams, there on the mound where my father had stopped the dump truck, the back rising into the night.

No one tried to interfere, stunned and standing very quiet in the bleachers while that single mass of dead, white chickens slid in one hard mass to the ground. My father bucked the truck ahead a couple of times, making sure the box was empty, before easing it down real slow so that it blocked the view behind us as we drove away.

The moon was almost full and straight above us by the time we got back to Paul Cutney's, having taken a long route, crisscrossing the farm country. Paul's house was dark, but lights were on in all three chicken barns. "They never see night," my father said. "Creatures of the electric bulb, tricked into laying eggs twenty-four hours a day."

I thought for no good reason that we might go inside and let a half-dozen hens out, just to see what they'd do. I was still holding the rosary, dangling it over my wrist the way I'd seen old people do, a single bead pressed between forefinger and thumb. They'd go around the rosary like that, praying and praying, and when they were finished they'd kiss the crucifix, then begin all over again. My father saw the rosary, for the first time, I think, and the tiny flecks of moonlight glinting in the beads. He said, "Kneel with me here." He said, "Look at all those stars," and I did, at the aurora borealis, and suddenly I did not feel at all funny in Paul Cutney's front yard, listening to my father make perfect sense again, now that he was back in his element.

DEATH PARTS

I do not advertise as a taxidermist, but each year I take a little work, mostly local. Occasionally, a downstater will get lucky and shoot a trophy whitetail on the opener, and for the right price I will mount the buck's head, usually a ten-point or better. My reputation has spread these past few years, so I can choose and charge what I want. I always agree to work on an animal I've never held, dead or alive, or a freak of nature, like the pure white skunk that was caught in a neighbor's trap, the eyes oversized and deep blue.

A black bear is the only animal I refuse to touch with the knife, no matter how much money I am offered. They are not rare, and if you have connections there are private dumps in the U.P. where the bears are easily killed. Most evenings they wade out from the dark woods and move slowly through the avenues of junked cars in the high grass. Although my father never shot a bear with a rifle, he often watched them close up through the scope. Five straight years he arranged to hunt at the same dump. For a few days before he arrived the owner would empty pails of rotten fish and meat by the blind. "Smells something awful," the guy would boast over the phone, but he guaranteed the bears would be there in the half-light, and they always were, my father confirmed, they always were, repeating it as though he were ashamed by such certainty, by the bears' intractable greed for garbage. He never explained more than that why he passed the easy shots so often.

And I figured he'd pass again the first time he invited me to go with him. He had borrowed a VW Beetle while the station wagon was in the shop, and right before pulling out of the yard he said, "What the hell. Let's give them a chance," and he went back into the house for the bow and arrows and left the rifle right there on the kitchen table. I was fourteen and I remember how we drove down a long dirt road to its dead end, a cloud of dust continuing past into the tall weeds. Already in camouflage we both got out of the car and my father stopped real close to the side mirror, uncapped his small tin of cream and began to smear black streaks across his cheeks and forehead. "You won't be with me in the blind," he explained. "I've got a spot for you to watch from. You'll see fine from there, and it's safer." He paused, then he said, "Take these," and swung me the binoculars by the cracked leather strap. I hung them around my neck while he strapped on his holster and pistol, and we started walking in. I was surprised how close the dump was from where we parked. It looked like a dried-up swamp, the low land curving in a half circle around the perimeter of trees, the maples deep orange and yellow at the far edge, the sumac blood red. The clearing was not large, about five acres. I expected the ground to be soft, but it wasn't when we stepped down and circled the pile of old refrigerators and washing machines and electric stoves, the white enamel rusted in small circles wherever a bullet had passed through.

The odor of fish hung thick in the air. "That's ripe," my father said, as he might while checking tomatoes in the garden. But it was more than ripe, here in the late fall, the nights already cold and heavy with frost. I thought about dump pickers who scavenged for a harvest of old bottles and ink wells and the porcelain heads of dolls in places just like this. But I couldn't imagine anyone digging in this stink for treasures, as I couldn't imagine why my father hunted every year over piles of entrails and fish heads. It was illegal to bait an area, and maybe that's why my father could never shoot these bears, haunted as he was by their desperate and voracious hunger. Or maybe just breathing this awful air made him sick of the woods after a few hours, crouched there and staring, one time in so sudden a snow the bears came in and were gone before he had seen them, like ghosts. He'd come close, he said, but he never fired, as he did so willingly at every other animal he'd ever hunted.

Halfway across he stopped and pointed toward a stand of popples about fifty yards ahead. "The blind's in there. You'll see it better from the cars." And I did, the sun setting behind me as I looked out the windshield of a 1949 Studebaker after my father slammed down the hood. "Look at that," he said smiling, showing me the dipstick through the open window. "She didn't die from lack of oil." And the seats too were pretty good, no broken springs poking through the gray upholstery. I imagined driving this car, the knee-high grass folding under the flaking chrome bumper on the zigzag of a final ride. But when I tried the steering wheel, it wouldn't budge, the bald tires buried to the hubcaps.

"Keep both doors locked and don't get out. If you have to pee, go right on the floor. I'll come get you after dark when it's time to leave." Then he took the pistol from his holster, and handle first, gave me the gun. It was a .32 caliber, too small to ever kill a bear, but it was loaded, and I took careful aim with the safety on as my father walked away, covering him until he reached the blind, believing at that moment no shot was out of range.

But accuracy is at least half luck when the light changes and the eyes strain too hard to make out shapes that aren't even there in the distance. Vision adjusts some, but still plays tricks enough to turn the mind to other things. Like jumping back to the first evening I plowed the garden under by myself, and stopped on the last row by the fenceline to place a few rotten pumpkins on the tops of the posts and, from the seat of the tractor, reached out and fired point blank on my way to the barn, the soft orange seeds exploding into a halo below the full moon. And that's the way memory is shattered. You are drifting in the past, but some primitive part of you is always alert to the killing urge of only the present moment.

I can't remember what I was thinking when that single bear, lumbering on all fours, angled in front of me, the momentum of her hind end carrying her whole body sideways toward the blind. I rolled down the window just a few inches to listen, at first leaning my ear against the cold air. But hearing nothing after a few minutes, I opened the door and, with both elbows steadied on the hood, I focused, not on the path of the bear, but to the left where my father was standing at full draw, the satellite razor head catching a shred of light the instant he released. I shifted the binoculars as though I could follow the flight of the arrow, the landscape made crazy through the tinted blue lenses by the sudden leap. Out of the high cover the bear charged into clear view and was heading toward me, her enormous bulk low to the ground, her head in a kind of slow motion lolling from side to side. My father told me later he heard the door slam, the noise that might have brought the bear stumbling to the driver's side where she lifted on her hind feet, her undersides moist and shiny with blood. The bright yellow fletching of the arrow stuck out above her breastbone, dead center at the base of the throat, the jugular and windpipe severed.

Unlike an .06 or a 30.30, it's the cutting of the razor tip that kills, not the impact. She would have died right there from loss of blood and no air, but when she stared in, narrow-eyed, her hot breath rising, I fired six times through the glass at her

face until she turned away into the green space of the field
and collapsed for good. The aluminum arrow shaft pointed
straight up into the widest gray I had ever seen absorbed so
quickly by the stars. They shone by the thousands a few
minutes later when my father arrived, silent and ready. He
had notched a second arrow, and shaking a little as he strad-
dled the steamy body, he drove the arrow deep into the sky,
the constellation of the bears glowing brighter and brighter
above us. When my father turned the bear over on her back, I
pointed them out and he said, without looking up, "Well this
one's dead!" and he bent down on one knee with his big knife
drawn, the tips of the fur so silver where he grabbed a hand-
ful and lifted the loose flesh for the blade I had honed that
morning, for this crime we could only cover up by taking the
body home.

Each night has its own trajectory, and star gazing north
above the hills, I offered my father no help, nor did he ask
until he stood up, stiff-legged, his forearms covered with
blood. "Get the towel from my bag," he said. I did, but instead of wiping his hands he wrapped it around the arrow,
and using the full power of his legs and back, he wrenched it
out, the bear's head lifting momentarily off the ground as if
she were staring at her empty belly. The long tail of a shooting star endured a few seconds of darkness and was gone.
Bear spirit, I thought, abstracting the image to legend or
folklore or myth that made the bear almost human, her arms
outstretched in that ugly, vulnerable pose of surrender.

It took a long time to drag her back to the car, my father
wheezing, always forcing himself a few steps too far before a
rest, his palms rope-burned and blistered. I stayed a ways in
front, carrying the bow and binoculars and empty gun. But
after about a half hour he yelled, "Get rid of that stuff and
bring back the gloves from the trunk." He lit a cigarette and I
could hear him coughing real bad, coughing and spitting. I
stopped and looked back from the edge of the dump. The
night was bright and quiet, and although it was cold now, I
could feel the sweat on my back. I reached under the layers of

clothes and pulled my T-shirt a couple of times away from my skin.

My father must have squared up again against the weight of the bear and, exhausted, he must have lost his grip on the rope and gone down hard, face first, and with that second wind of rage, shouted at the top of his lungs, "You bitch, you filthy whore," that last word a kind of groan, raspy in his throat, the savage note of hatred taking control.

I hurried back with a cold beer from the cooler. It was still wet from the ice and my father squeezed it between his hands. "I'm okay," he said, calm now. "We'll get her out." And together we did, the rope lengthened and tied around his waist, hands on his hips, almost casual except for the strain on those thick legs, farmer's legs for hauling calves from the muck, or for dragging a wagon load of hay a few inches in the field to the trailer hitch of the tractor. My legs were thin and long like a sprinter's, like my mother's he had once said, to run ahead in the night for cans of beer and gloves and for the quick distance my father sometimes needed from me to think things out and make sure what he was teaching me was exactly what I needed to know.

Getting her up and lashed on top of the VW was easier than I'd expected. She seemed to slide backwards up the smooth roundness of the hood. I pushed on her shoulders, and my father, stretching from the rear bumper, locked her huge back paws under his armpits and, leaning back, he hauled her over the windshield to the roof, a filmy streak of blood coating the glass. The Volkswagen was yellow and she seemed big enough to crush it in a bear hug. We stood back and watched a minute, then cut four lengths of rope and tied her down in that ridiculous pose. I needed sleep, and drifting off I imagined I was inside her belly as my father started driving toward the main road, craving a hamburger, he said, someplace well lighted where the bear would be safe in the parking lot while we chowed down on the "Early Bird Special." He was attracted, he said, to the scent of a particular all-night diner, the waitresses so clean and pretty and always asking if he'd had any luck, and him spinning halfway around this time on the counter stool to point out the window, and me nodding yes beside him, nodding real slow over the spread menu like someone with an appetite.

The car broke down on the long deserted stretch through the Hiawatha National Forest. The radio was all static. I woke up hot in the sleeping bag, the red cotton lining patterned with deer. I asked my father the time and he said, "About 2:00 A.M." He had just come from the rear of the car.

"What's the matter?"

"We started losing pressure a few miles back. There's no power left. Must have labored too hard under this load."

He knew engines, but hated the foreign jobs. "Piece of crap," he said, "but what do you expect with the motor in the ass end?" I was back there with him this time as he reached in without a light, the way he had reached into the entrails of the bear, and when he pulled his hands out they were covered with oil. "Can't drive it," he said. "We're stuck until someone comes by."

But nobody did and every now and then he would pump up the Coleman lantern until the new mantle glowed white inside the glass. Then he'd place it on the side of the road like a flare and walk off into the blackness. The lantern threw a lot of light into the pines, and it made the blood smear on the windshield very dark. I got out once and noticed for the first time that the bear's eyes were wide open, angry from the bite of the wind.

"I'll close them," my father said, frightening me from behind. He did it so gently with his thumbs, saddened I think, by so little control of the dead who stare back at the awful times before we can put them to rest.

"Did you bait him or get him with dogs?" the guy in the wrecker asked. "He's bigger than the damn car!" In the daylight I could see that the whole front of the yellow VW was covered with blood. "Didn't clean him out too good," the guy continued. "We got a hose you can use at the station. Shove the nozzle right down his throat and rinse him out good before the meat spoils."

I corrected him: "It's a her." He was missing half of his middle finger on the right hand and the stub was stained dark with nicotine.

"Then we'll do her from the other end," he said, and flicked his unfinished cigarette up at the bear and began manhandling the chains and harness and yanked back a lever that released the main cable from the spool on the wrecker. Then, grunting a little, he took off his greasy baseball cap and crawled part way under the car, his pants low under his fat stomach, his legs spread on the gravel, spread wide enough for an easy kick to the balls. I might have taken a step closer, but probably not. "Ain't much to hook onto," the guy yelled back, but he came right out and the car went up easy on its rear wheels, the bear sliding back a bit on the roof. The three of us rode in the cab of the wrecker, me squeezed in the middle. There was a crime magazine on the floor, a naked woman gagged and tied by her wrists and ankles to the bedposts. Seeing it, my father wedged the magazine under the seat with the heel of his boot, and the guy, shifting into third and staring into the side and rearview mirrors, shook his homely head and pulled out with the emergency flashers pulsing down the miles of empty road.

"It's your lucky day," the guy started up. "We've got a VW wreck at the station. Had to tow it back on a flatbed. It's a fucking mess right to the rear seat, but the engine's untouched. Two people killed. You can hardly sell parts from a car like that. Too much superstition about robbing the dead. The dead!" He laughed and shook his head and paused to let that sink in. "You don't believe in that shit, do you?"

"I don't," I said too quickly, but my father, eyes closed and head tilted back against the rear window, asked, "How does anyone know?"

"I know," the guy snapped. "Sure as shit I know," and for several minutes after that he went silent.

My father said later that the guy was full of it, a big talker hero. But there was something frightening about the way he punched the radio buttons with that half finger and talked on and on about how he got people's attention "right now" when he flipped them the stubby bird. At the station we helped him push the VW, the bear still on top, into the service bay. The customer bell rang as a car pulled away from the gas pumps out front, and the young gas attendant carrying a five-dollar bill stepped from the sunlight and asked my father, "How much you want for the claws?"

"They're not for sale," my father answered. But I knew they were a couple hours later when the tow guy handed us the bill. He had written DEATH PARTS for everything he had stripped from the wreck. And knowing we couldn't pay, he sent the car up on the lift as if to keep it out of reach, the bear on top rising in grotesque ascension into the brutal darkness bunched under the roof.

"Let's talk turkey," the guy said, his sermon of harsh facts. He looked mean now. "I'll take fifty bucks and the bear."

While they dickered I walked outside and sat down on the concrete abutment at the base of the Texaco sign. Toward what there was of a town hung a blinking yellow light, suspended and swinging a little from a wire across the road. Just that single color, and beyond, the huge white numbers on the water tower: Pop. 412. I could hear the air brakes of a transport trailer slowing for the light, then shifting through his gears and moving pretty good by the time he passed me. I ducked my head from the sudden draft and noise and I could smell the dirty cattle for a long time after the truck was out of sight.

When I started back my father was at the pumps washing blood from the windshield of the VW, and behind him, the silhouette of the bear hanging by her neck, the rope fastened to one runner of the lift. The guy and the kid were already spreading her claws, spreading them and laughing as she swayed, her toes a few inches off the ground.

"Maybe they would take the binoculars," I suggested. My

father, exhausted from no sleep, nodded but got into the VW and said, "Let's go home," and tested the car's top end down that long straightaway. But he slowed after a few miles, sensing, I guess, the danger of traveling in such a small car. "Death parts," he whispered to himself, then put the head-lights on at high noon and pulled close to the right shoulder of the road whenever another vehicle passed, heading the other way.

FLEA TO JESUS

The DNR, assessing the damage to the fruit trees, said okay to the farmers, hire someone, and they did. They hired my father who had been temporarily laid off from his regular job. They knew that although he hadn't hunted in years, he was the best with a rifle, and that for as long as they had known him, he always needed money. They made it legal for him to shoot all the deer he could, and from anywhere—a car, a tree stand, and at any time, even by shining if that produced results fast.

The DNR officers who handed him the permit said, "No questions. Just cull the herd." The same urgency was apparent, though angrier, when Orly Thayer, staring across his four hundred acres and speaking for the Farmers' Collective, said, "Kill the bastards before we all go broke." My father had already failed at farming ten years earlier and he just nodded, accepting the job of bounty hunter.

It was March, milder finally, and half-starved from six months of winter, the deer were leaving the yards to browse the new growth of apple and cherry, and I had just turned seventeen. The guidance counselor at the high school said absolutely, I'd be offered a full ride to U of M, but my father was making sure a year and a half in advance, covering what he called the hidden expenses behind every generous hand-out. So he brought the rifles out, reducing the hunt to profit, something he'd preached against his whole life. But now his equations were simple—a carcass was worth so much of a history or religion credit or a physics textbook or the price of a chamber recital, something he said he'd never attend, but what the hell, that was college these days and I should take in the whole shooting match. "No pun intended," he said smiling, obedient now to the intelligence of such a risk-free investment in my future.

The next day he walked and walked the orchards, not with his .06, but with a pad and pencil, and that evening over dinner he began talking "damage ratio," calculating how many deer needed to be removed (that's the word he used) from each area. "Removed" sounded as though he intended to trap them live or tranquilize them with darts. I imagined the deer, thin and groggy, breathing heavily in the back of the station wagon. Maybe they'd even struggle to their knees, then fall over hard each time my father swerved intentionally, watching them in the rearview mirror, watching for their narrow faces to rise again above the rear seat. But there'd be none of that, no transporting them to another county where they'd wake clear-eyed under the stars. He meant to kill them all right, and he said make no mistake about it, which I didn't, though I sensed he'd pay for what he did, and in some other way, I'd pay too.

"What will they do with the deer?" I asked, and my father said, "They'll process the meat and take it up to the asylum." Already something seemed crazy, the deer so weak and vulnerable, and I remembered how the patients stared down at me one time from behind those barred windows at dusk, the same way I'd be staring down soon from Angus McCoskey's loft door in his barn, silent and waiting for something terrible to occur.

There had been talk a couple years back about my father being put away, but that all passed and no one mentioned his rampaging anymore, not even the kids at school. But I could detect his craziness coming on, remote and dimensionless, though definitely there, circling just out of range. And I knew any insinuation to scrap this plan would only bring the craziness on. That scared me more than anything in the world, so I talked to him about winterkill and the necessity of deer control and on and on that way, as though the accuracy of logic could drop madness in its tracks.

We drove out together to Angus McCoskey's cherry farm. Angus was a man who had turned to God the very day his wife of forty-seven years died of a stroke in the orchard. She died with pruning shears still clutched in her hands. "Literally," my father had told me, "they had to pry her fingers apart." Now Angus saw each tree as a shrine. He said that to my father while the three of us stood a few minutes on his back porch, our rifles still in their cases. He said every time the orchard turned white with petals he was reminded of Easter, the resurrection, the sacredness of this life in the country. And he said finally that the eating frenzy of deer each spring was a desecration, and he wanted them dead. He called them devils, but I knew there was something haywire with that notion, something contemptible in the way we were taking such fierce aim at hunger, as though we had a covenant beyond the name of conservation.

Angus had painted, in blocked red letters across the side of his whitewashed barn, FLEA TO JESUS. Had the misspelling been deliberate, I might have thought him a deep thinker, a holy man, interpreting the boundaries of the universe: the minuscule and the sublime, the temporary and the everlasting. I thought how I might work the three words of his phrase into an essay for an advanced class in philosophy or theology, subjects I wanted to study in college.

But for now, I'd spend time learning to kill for money in Angus McCoskey's loft, where my father pushed open the door with his foot, and gave me the word: "Load up." Then he said, "Angus McCoskey's a fanatic. He's got a cow's name." If my father was making a connection, I didn't get it, but his tone was derisive, as though he'd listened too long and too often to the scriptures of lunatics, people you might meet in a madhouse, preaching about the Second Coming, or about just rewards. My father felt his just rewards were way over-due, so when the first few deer angled across the open space of the orchard from the swamp, he didn't hesitate, taking up the whole space of the door, so I couldn't even get sighted to fire. Nor did he repent on the drive home, nor later when we hung his first buck in years upside down from the rafters in the garage. We'd left three others, another buck, though much smaller, and two does, for the DNR. My father had shot them all.

In bed, after my homework, I imagined I could almost read the illegible scrawl of blood in the snow, something like "savior" or "survive," a single word with s's and v's and r's, and I thought then of "visor," and the blue-and-white button my father had pinned in the car, the button that said, IN GOD'S IMAGE, that perfection to which the human kind willed its existence. I liked FLEA TO JESUS much better. It seemed to attach some discomfort to God, as though He too, like all beasts of the field, was kept scratching. I would never have said that to my father, nor to Angus McCoskey, who believed God gave us dominion over every living thing on this earth, to name and to kill—that interpretation.

I was not sacrilegious when I was seventeen. I attended Mass and made confession often. When I was still in elemen-tary school, I had made my First Communion and Confirma-tion, and I attended catechism Saturday mornings at the Holy Cross Parish without missing a single time for a full year, learning Christianity from the nuns. I was always fascinated most by those people in the Bible who said "no," those disciples of wariness, like Adam and Lot's wife, who tempted the blind-faith doctrine of God. Maybe I was doing that too, blaspheming my way to eternal damnation with all my crazy thoughts and speculations, like how religion and insanity were a little bit the same, a threat and a refuge. It seemed that way a lot, especially when listening to Angus McCoskey, who, right before we drove away, recited the opening of the Benedictus, translating the Latin for us. He said, as though addressing our killing mission, "Blessed is He that cometh in the name of the Lord." I was glad my father did not say, "Amen." I did not want him agreeing with anything out there, nor believing for one minute that we should be redeemed for what we'd done that evening from our outpost in the barn.

My father said we'd be back at work same time tomorrow to get the others. I didn't know how many that was, nor how long we'd spend trying to fill that quota. I wanted to move on to someplace else where at least we'd be alone, just the two of us, less aware of God. My father, sensing my uneasiness, calmed me down when he said, "Good Jesus, protect us all from lunatics like Angus McCoskey."

And that's what I thought about, my father's good sense, before I finally fell asleep, having already said my prayers on my knees, out loud, in a way I hadn't done for years, asking forgiveness for the way my mind sometimes played tricks with those higher laws of the Cross, the ones I'd been instructed over and over never to doubt. And then I asked for the spirits of those four deer to be saved, and the ones we'd kill tomorrow, and the next day, and the next, meaning them no harm.

My father went out by himself before daylight and, when I got home from school, he was in the garage, working up the deer, getting the hide off. He'd been over to Derald Salensky's all morning, slow-walking the orchards in a light snow, no wind. He still seemed okay, though a little distant when he mentioned "Blood Angels," referring to the deep impressions the fallen deer left in the snow. I wanted to ask him how many he killed, not to tally up the earnings, but to keep track for my prayers at night, and for the candles I promised myself I'd light one night in Holy Cross Church: red candles, maybe four or five rows of them, a whole herd's worth, a congregation of deer. That image seemed holy, as church always did, especially those times I was the only one there, alone at the altar at night. It was strange, I guess, how I didn't pray much under that huge, deep-grained crucifix, not "Our Fathers" and "Hail Marys" anyway, nothing with real words, nothing memorized by easy sound and cadence. Until I saw the "Lord's Prayer" written out one day, I thought "Hallowed be Thy" was a single word—the Lord's name, Halobeethy. So I composed my own prayers after that, not in verse, not in any language you could transcribe. Perhaps it wasn't prayer at all, not in a church sense, but more a meditation. Whenever I'd close my eyes in that state, I'd drift, for what seemed like miles, into silence. I imagined, at those times, if I were a cripple or a mute or a leper, I would dance or sing a canticle or offer my cheek to a beautiful woman to kiss. That feeling. Nothing less.

I don't know why my father never asked me about school, but he didn't, not ever. Maybe it was because he couldn't help me with diagramming sentences or with translating Spanish to English, or maybe it was because I always got straight A's and, after all these years, he simply expected that. But he'd stare at those grades a long time before signing my report card, as though he was reluctant to give it up. And he'd nod a lot, too, easy nods, and sometimes he'd tutor me on the meaning of leverage—how I could tip the world in my favor if I studied hard, if I had faith in God and landed a full scholarship to the university. He said no amount of OT or second jobs or dead deer could ever balance the weight of a college degree, not only in dollars and cents but, more importantly, in the quality of a man's life. "Guaranteed," he said. "Mark it down. Remember it for good!"

He'd only made it to the eleventh grade at the parochial school, but he was sharp in other ways—incisive, cynical—

though he spoke to himself in a tone, his lips moving, that other people figured was just nonsense-muttering. I remember, one day in the fourth grade, how my teacher, maybe just funning around, said to the class, "People who talk to themselves have money in the bank." That was the first time I ever heard that, and I didn't even raise my hand. I shouted out, "That's a lie and a lie's a sin." Ricky Christianson, that do-gooder, laughed and turned around in his seat and, for the rest of the day in silent mimicry, mouthed those words at me: "That's a lie and a lie's a sin." But I knew I was right. My father was broke and being broke was one of the things that drove him nuts and got him muttering in public in the first place, sometimes while browsing the aisles of the A&P, eating grapes and cherries, as though he were testing their quality in the field right before harvest, the whole time dictating strategies to survive setbacks and losses, strategies so complicated only he could decipher them. When nobody listened, he'd go berserk after a while, usually after we got home from shopping. He'd say scary things about criminals in local politics, and about religion and God, things I knew he didn't mean for good, things he'd forbidden me ever to say under any conditions. And I'd run away and hide in the barn for hours, and I wouldn't cry for fear he'd find me.

I never learned how to prevent his crack-ups, how to intervene early and stave off the madness. I did learn to recognize the symptoms coming on and, at seventeen, I knew I wouldn't run frightened from his craziness. Anyhow, lately he'd been much better, but years earlier he'd explode at any time, and without warning. It got so bad and so frequent that he'd seen a psychiatrist—he had to. The court ruled I, too, should attend the sessions (that's what the judge called them) once a month for a full year. The psychiatrist prescribed tranquilizers for my father, which he flushed down the toilet, two pills each day. He reported back each Friday afternoon that the medication was doing the trick, relaxing him real good. The psychiatrist said most likely my father was fighting a chemical imbalance, something about extra chromosomes. It sounded dirty to me, like a sex problem, and I hated that quack, his big-shot degrees framed on the wall behind his desk. There was no chance I'd ever enter that field, no matter how much it paid, brainwashing people who were confused enough already, filling their heads with junk like that.

And I hated the way he condescended to my father, calling him a devout Catholic who needed only to tame his "incendiary spirit." I asked my father later what that meant. He said he'd already looked it up a couple weeks back. He said, "I guess sometimes I breathe a lot of fire." We laughed and shook our heads in the car, figuring it was the shrink who had the screw loose with all his fancy terminology, playing the savior, wanting us to bow down in gratitude for his miraculous cures.

"How is madness hereditary?" I asked my father. The psychiatrist had said it was, like hair color or the color of eyes.

"It's all hogwash," my father said, and I said back, "That's for sure," in the calm ritual of agreement, the blood therapy between fathers and sons. My father's eyes were dark brown, nothing like mine, and he had been nearsighted since he was a little kid. My vision was twenty-twenty. And anyway, I knew nobody could foresee the future, nobody but God, and lately He hadn't sent me any real clear signs to make me worry, nothing maybe, except FLEA TO JESUS, though that seemed more a riddle than a warning.

My father acted calm, as sane as any man who went quietly about his work, keeping regular hours without complaint or too many beers at the end of the day. He did not seem at all bothered by the crazy nature of this new job, what the timid might call a bloodbath or slaughter, those who couldn't possibly understand this kind of mercy, how killing so much could ever be a decent thing.

If it got to my father, I couldn't detect it even after the first full week. He'd reduced the herd by twenty-eight. I saw that in his record book. It read: "12 Bucks + 16 Does = 28 deer =

$560.00 = The Future!" Then he transferred that sum to the next page under the heading COLLEGE FUND. That was more than twice the amount he made each week at the Fisk, much of it working the graveyard shift, though before being laid off, he'd been back on days. And as he pointed out, the bounty dollars were tax free, wages paid under the table. And suddenly there were bonuses, incentives from Angus McCoskey, who called late that second Sunday night, waking my father to tell him to scrap that quota bullshit. He said the deer were back. I imagined them floating from tree to tree in darkness, like a blight. My father said no a bunch of times, exhausted no's. He was edgy and wanted to get off the phone. His eyes were bloodshot, and he was coughing a lot, covering the mouthpiece with his hand.

I was still up studying at the kitchen table, rereading "Higher Laws," my favorite chapter from *Walden*, and going over my notes for a test next morning. I whispered, "Hang up," and my father did finally, but not before agreeing to return one more time, saying his quota system was based on a "give-or-take-a-few philosophy" anyway, and that a guy just starting out in business like this had to allow for a certain leeway. I knew Angus McCoskey must have offered him a lot of money for my father to change his mind like that, and I said, "It's not worth it, whatever he'll pay. That's too many deer." Looking back, just before he closed his bedroom door, he gave me the first indication that he could snap at anytime. He said, quoting Angus McCoskey, "We must aspire to rid the Christian world of such vermin." Coming from my father's mouth, it was the strangest mandate I'd ever heard.

The next morning he told me he sweated all night, and I was relieved, thinking he'd been delirious in fever when he said what he did. He was so sick that I skipped school and waited for Dr. Wozniak, who said it was the Asian flu, a miserable strain, the worst he'd seen, and what my father had to do now was rest. He did. He slept the whole day while I read in the kitchen and, when he awakened, I told him I was on my way to Angus McCoskey's to finish up, and he said, "The wages of sin," and I said back, "If they're high enough, maybe it's okay this time, just this once."

"Maybe," he said, in that disquieting monotone of disbelievers too tired to argue. "Maybe so, but who cares? I already feel like hell."

On the drive over I thought how easy it is sometimes to manipulate the conscience, to vindicate ourselves, at least for a little while, of all that guilt religion breeds in the soul. My father *did* feel like hell, barraged, not so much by the flu, but by that Job syndrome of taking it hard on the chin, suffering the love of reduction, the love of a wrecked life, over and over and then simply writing it off for God. At some point a guy figured it was all a crock, that he deserved better, and if a greater rivalry existed later on, well let it come, but for now all faith was suspended. Maybe that was the riddle of FLEA TO JESUS, how we revered one extreme and then the other, pagan and saint.

I did not park in Angus McCoskey's driveway. I parked instead on the side of the road by the swamp and left my gun case in the back seat and followed the deer run along the orchard's edge, then cut back straight to the barn, undetected. I hadn't asked my father; I just took his .06 with the illuminator scope. The day had been clear, and there would be a full moon and, if I decided to, I could shoot all night, for as long as the deer were in sight. I pushed open the loft door with my foot, just as my father had—I got that far—and I loaded the clip and scanned the orchard on 8-power, whispering, "Bam, bam," sighting those imaginary deer the mind summons in preparation for the real kill. "Spare none of them," Angus McCoskey had said that first evening, and I, a disbeliever in greed, had returned in the name of Money, that newest god my father trusted would deliver me from the graceless routines of this small town, its small-minded teachings. Even the humor of FLEA TO JESUS had worn thin. But I wasn't convinced that the teachings of Ann Arbor would be less futile, any less confused. Maybe that was the world, a succession of foreign tongues, lopsided spiels on the origin and spirit of man.

All I knew for sure was that the first skinny deer appeared like an apparition, almost white in the full moonlight of the orchard. And just above the trees, an incandescence like a halo, the night so bright shadows moved across the snow, shadows of deer, eight or ten now, passing on their way from starvation, trespassing, as Angus McCoskey would have seen it, against him, against the will of Jesus. And I was *not* there to resist the temptation to kill, or to sanctify a queasy conscience, the safety off, each deer moving broadside through the cross hairs. So I fired, and when I ran downstairs and outside, my hood pushed back, I felt the pulse of the stars, as though the night itself had been frightened by the sudden noise.

A few minutes later, on Angus McCoskey's back porch, the light blinked on, and I imagined him just inside the door, counting bonus dollars. But I couldn't collect. I couldn't find the deer, or blood angels in the snow, or a trail of blood to follow. My father always said too much adrenaline could do that, cause even the best marksman to miss the easy shots, which I did, perhaps jerking the trigger or closing my eyes at the last instant. But I couldn't help feeling that something else had interceded. I didn't know what. Scared, I began to run when Angus McCoskey shouted my father's name, wanting to bless and pay me, I guess, but I wouldn't stop, my legs pushing and pushing me, like anything mortal and desperate to survive.

PART 2

THE SEASON OF FAMILIES

Jack O'Conner is a pharmacist who is right now on his way to upstate New York to visit his father for the holidays. He has brought some sample packs of vitamins for him to try, a whole bagful, and small silver tubes of ointments for his father's stubborn neck rash. And for himself, a sample pack of condoms. Red, white, and blue ones, which might be comical to someone with a more fluid sense of humor. His wife, Eartha, is forty-four, five years older than Jack, and he has just recently stopped supplying her with birth control pills. They're for younger women, as Jack says, and Eartha thinks, yes, for the sixteen-year-olds he hires to work Saturdays for minimum wage. Until last year, Eartha worked three afternoons a week at Dove Song, a local flower shop. Since the recession, she has been unemployed. They have no children and want none and Jack's father has begun to refer to this as their selfishness. Which it is. But unlike most of their married friends, they are companionable enough and spend freely and, as Jack points out, without worry. They travel on his vacations, often by plane to exotic places, he always in an aisle seat in nonsmoking, she way in the back by the bathrooms.

Eartha has carefully wrapped the Christmas presents in shiny silver paper and blue stick-on bows from the drugstore. The presents are stacked on the back seat of their Saab turbo which is parked again on the icy shoulder of Highway 23, this time between two long white fields. Eartha is sitting cross-legged on the front bumper, the wind gusting in miniature tornadoes of new snow through the barbed-wire fence to her right. That's why she's holding her coat collar up higher on that side of her face, and smoking faster than normal.

Jack, who is not impatient, believes that these are sugar beet fields, a major crop of mid-Michigan, where Eartha was born and raised and attended a community college, majoring in pre-med. Those dreams are long done for. Jack uses sugar beets to bait the deer he hunts every fall with bow and arrow in the woods behind their house. He has venison steaks which Eartha, a vegetarian, will not eat, frozen in a styrofoam cooler in the trunk. But Jack's father, a retired stock broker, will, and has asked for some prime cuts, calling it deer meat. It's leaner, he claims, than anything he can buy in the markets, which is not, as he puts it, small potatoes to a man who has survived a second heart attack and now pays close attention to his cholesterol. Jack knows that twenty-two percent of Michigan residents can tell you their cholesterol level, the most informed state in the country. Wisconsin has the highest binge drinking rate, by far the worst obesity. New York the most sedentary life-style. He bores Eartha with facts like these—this man who stands all day behind a glass partition in his long white coat, surrounded by plastic pull-out bins of pills he believes can cure most people's ills.

Jack knows nothing of Eartha's addiction to Valium, a prescription she gets filled in Mancelona, a twenty-minute drive from where they live. For this trip she has hidden the Valium in a metal Sucrets box, spread under the top layer of lozenges. She wishes her doctor would prescribe something stronger, especially for family visits. But, as he's explained, she's already at maximum dosage, already, as she knows, fading in and out of most days.

She dislikes Jack's father who referred to her once, trying to talk his only son out of the marriage, as "either incredibly dense or catatonic." Eartha heard this while eavesdropping on the portable telephone in the basement. Which is what she did again a few nights ago, listening this time to her father-in-law read Jack the riot act about her smoking in his "home." He'd consented finally to this much—she can do it only on the new screened-in porch out back. "Any place," she said later to Jack. "Wherever."

On their only other visit since their marriage six years ago, the temperature outside near zero, she had gotten quietly out of bed that first night, Jack snoring lightly, and had opened the window in the upstairs guest room just an inch, and pressed her lips right tight to the crack each time she exhaled through the screen. She remembers, in the cold hazy moonlight of the backyard, how the neighbor's black-and-white Great Dane had stared up at her, and how much it had resembled a zebra, her all-time favorite animal, standing knee-deep in the snow. Mercy, she had thought, a zebra, but she did not wake Jack, certain that he would understand this scene exactly for what it was—her sneaking cigarettes and watching a big dog let out to go to the bathroom. The bathroom she and Jack shared was right down the carpeted hallway, and she tip-toed there, carrying her shoe, the one she had used as an ashtray. She emptied the ashes, and the butts snubbed out above the filters, into the toilet and flushed.

And she could not imagine, the next morning, how Jack's father knew. But he did. He was in his bathrobe and slippers, sitting alone at the kitchen table when she walked in, still headachy from the long drive and the late cocktails and way too little sleep. He did not offer her coffee, which is what she had craved, strong black coffee. That and a cigarette. When she said, "Good morning," and smiled at him, he stood slowly and pointed at her and said back, "Eartha, my wife died from lung cancer and, goddamnit, I'll rent you a room at the Ramada if that's what it takes to keep you from lighting up in here, in my house. Yes," he said, "mine, and I make the rules, like it or not." He paused, and then he said, "And I'll tell you something, just between you and me. You're trouble," and he started to say something else, but clenched his teeth instead and walked away.

She'd felt nabbed, as though he'd been waiting there for her since before sun-up, his lips taut with an anger she had known other men to have. Her own father, for one, who slapped her hard across the face that first time he discovered a pack of Kents in her bedroom. He made her open her mouth and breathe her tobacco breath at him. Tramp, he had called her. Little tart-whore. She was thirteen and had just gotten out of the shower, rosy-skinned and nothing on but a bath towel wrapped around her, her hair dripping wet. Because of her lankiness, the frayed edge of the towel hung only a little ways down her thighs. He did not even allow her to get dressed, though she had cried and then shivered badly. For almost an hour she stood there, chain-smoking the entire pack in front of him, her mother walking meekly in after a while and sitting at the foot of the bed, her hands composing themselves into prayer on her lap. "Sweetheart," her mother had said when they were alone. "Sweetheart, please. Please obey your father. He knows what's best for you. He does." Followed a few days later by her mother's secret inducements if Eartha would only give up the smoking—a new baton, private cello lessons—all kid's stuff. So she remained unrepentent, the nicotine stains darkening between her fingers. She always hated her father after that, hated the single-minded wrath of any man laying down the law for her.

Jack was different—soft spoken, encouraging rather than condemning her. She can't remember how many gimmicks he has brought home over the years to help her quit—over-the-counter gums, then Nicorette, then thin, long-filtered cigarettes that tasted like air. She knows what she lacks is will power, which is why, one night while Jack was in Chicago at a pharmaceutical convention, she had slept with his best friend, a man named Lyman Clark. It had not been her intention to do this, nor his, when he knocked on the wooden frame of the screen door. It was summer then and she undid the hook latch and stepped back, wearing a thin nightgown and, except for her panties, nothing underneath. A fan whirred at high speed from the corner of the kitchen, and Lyman was holding a cold beer to his forehead and inquiring as to Jack's whereabouts, and then only nodding and staring. She does not remember it being good or bad, but only that it happened. And again a few months later, what Lyman described as a relapse. But he phoned the next day saying that he was sick about it, nauseous. When he returned a third time, she wouldn't let him in. The three of them are not often together anymore, but whenever they are, Lyman seems jumpy and afraid. Jack, of course, does not notice.

At this moment he is consumed by the details of automobile navigation, the road map spread across the steering wheel. As long as Eartha has known him, he has never once gotten them lost. So it seems strange to her when a car stops to ask if they are all right. No, she wants to tell the woman on the passenger side. For the love of Christ, no. But it is Jack who answers and thanks them and waves by saluting with his left hand.

Jack, having figured in the cigarette breaks, one every fifty-five miles, like the speed limit, says, "We're making good time." Eartha nods and snaps a Kleenex from the cellophane pack on the dashboard. She wipes her nose, then presses her fingers between her knees. Jack turns up the heater a notch and turns the Lumbar knob to tighten the back of his seat, his solution to achy vertebrae. Even after a morning's worth of driving and stopping there are no grievances to air. Over the years, routines have taken hold. Jack simply says, "Onward," and shifts into first gear, and Eartha, the cold still deep insider her clothes, says, "Yes."

Eartha blanks out often, not knowing if Jack has talked, or if she has answered. She can will these trances, and does often, but this one is broken when Jack says, "Good God, look at that," and he points ahead and to his left. When Eartha leans forward she has to shade her eyes in order to see through the windshield a colossal blue silo with a Christmas tree on top. She wonders immediately from how far away on this flat land at night a person could see those blinking white lights if she were lost, that single star.

"Forever," Jack says, but he's talking about something else, about how long a man stays dead if he's not careful, decorating a tree that high up in the sky. Jack calculates, from the height of the house and the barn roof, that the silo must rise up at least a hundred feet. What interests Eartha is the angle at which the man, his arms outspread like a swan, would hit the frozen ground. She gives the man a face she recognizes— it is Jack's face, his light blue eyes, and now she cannot get that image out of her mind. He is wearing only one glove and no hat, and she is bending down to touch him, surrounded by all those cows. She thinks, maybe this is how it happens—a wife goes outside, calling and calling her husband back until she finds him dead. Eartha rarely feels the urge to touch Jack anymore, but she does that now, her fingertips soft on the back of his neck and, sorry for this vision she's created, she says, "Let's stop," says it as though she's asking for a motel room where they can draw the blinds against the late morning glare of the sun and make desperate and dangerous love.

Jack says, "Soon, there's a restaurant just up ahead." He says, "Hang on," and increases his speed by maybe five miles per hour. For a minute Eartha believes she is going to cry, and tears do come, but they do not leave her eyes, so that when she sees the giant, inflatable reindeer staked and wavering above the parking lot, the day seems even more unreal, blurry now, distorted. Eartha has lost her appetite for anything except a cigarette and another pill, her usual highway diet. Jack teases her at times like this, saying she should eat better and outlive him and collect on his net worth. It's a standing joke. Which is exactly what they are doing, standing. Both of them are, together in front of the car and staring up at the reindeer who smiles back down on them. Eartha is truly frightened. It strikes her that she is a small girl again and that she does not want to walk beneath this monstrous thing.

When she takes Jack's hand, it could be her father's, and what surges through her body is that adrenaline feeling that she is about to be yelled at, scolded, and hit again. She stands transfixed, unable to speak, her lips parted and heart-shaped as Jack—and yes, it is him—leans down to kiss her. And does, and he puts his arm around her shoulder and leads her safely to the door, which he opens for her, and then she feels his hand on the small of her back, guiding her into the vestibule. The inner door is glass and, as it closes behind her, she glances back. Jack is fumbling in his pockets for the right change to buy a newspaper from the yellow vending machine against the wall.

The restaurant is warm and knotty-pine and empty of any customers. And hanging from the scattered light fixtures, there are red-and-green crepe paper bells, the kind you can close-up and flatten and put away in a box until next Christmas. Although Eartha does not see a jukebox, she hears Willie Nelson's nasally version of "O, Holy Night." There are thousands of silver sparkles in the swirled, textured ceiling, because it is that kind of place, the waitress just this moment noticing Eartha and cracking a roll of quarters on the corner of the cash register drawer. She pushes the last few out with her thumb, and she says, "Smoking, hon?" as though there is no doubt. Eartha follows her and slides, without taking off her coat or scarf, into the corner of the booth bench. The waitress points out the Christmas week specials on the blackboard on the wall and says she'll be right back to take the order.

Eartha reads as far as the liver and onions, turning away again from the whole idea of food, turning instead to the window where she pulls open the wooden shutters. There is frost on the panes. And beyond, dwarfing the Saab in shadow, that awful reindeer.

She is startled by the glass of water the waitress sets down in front of her in the thin rectangle of light.

"No," Eartha says, she is not quite ready to order. She's sorry, but she still needs a couple minutes. She spends them, and more, locked in the stall in the ladies room. And this time she weeps openly, so hard she can taste the warm salt. For how long, she isn't sure. All she knows is that the cold tap water splashed on her face feels good. Then she brushes her hair and stares at her reflection in the mirror and decides she looks okay. It's not that she'll show no signs of this sadness, but she knows from experience, that from where Jack sits on the other side of the room, that he will not see that her eyes are red and puffy. Perhaps he'll not even look up from the sports page.

But he does this time, just as she sits back down, calmed already by another Valium and a cigarette she has lit with the very last match in the book. Jack keeps pointing outside, pointing beyond her, and she realizes at what when he cocks his right arm back and curls three fingers around an imaginary bow string, his thumb anchored on his ear lobe. He is taking aim at that reindeer floating there as big as a house. In his way, she thinks, he really has tried to destroy those beasts who possess her—the reason, of course, that she has stayed with him and, at moments like this, might even call it love.

But the waitress has seen it differently, and she bends down on one knee, her chin resting on her fist at the edge of the table, and she asks Eartha in a whisper if that guy over there is bothering her.

Sometimes, Eartha wants to say, and she almost tells the woman how often her fingers go numb by the roadsides, how many times she has eaten alone. Like now, she wants to say. Like this. She says instead, "No. No, he's not."

"Yuck," the waitress says, glancing back at Jack in his perfectly creased suntans and burgundy turtleneck and shiny new loafers. "Double yuck," she says, which sounds to Eartha like double yolk, Jack's standard late morning order—two eggs sunnyside up.

"Coffee," Eartha says, "please. Black coffee." And when it comes she presses both her hands around the cup. The restaurant is drafty, especially when a couple comes in, each smiling and carrying a blond-headed child. Nothing unusual in that. Just other travelers, Eartha suspects, in this the season of families.

THE WILDERNESS STATE

Hell is *not* room 101. I'd gladly come eyeball to eyeball with the goddamn rats. *Bring them on,* I thought, staring at a class of mine. *Bring the ugly bastards on!* But nobody will—*1984* is already old hat and the new hell is this latest stack of freshman essays.

The first one I read ends, *And this is what I think.* I want to write, *No shit,* and hand it back, but I don't. It's Weasel Conroy's essay on dying. He claims to have seen his father kill a man and dump the body in a bayou. Who knows, maybe he did. But it's unlikely, and if I were a priest instead of a teacher, someone more honest, and Weasel came to me for confession, I'd tell him that. Instead I write on the bottom of his last page, *Interesting,* one of the words I hate most in this garble of a world.

Weasel's from Louisiana. I haven't a clue what he's doing

at a technical college in northern Michigan nor, for that matter, what I'm doing here either. Teaching, if you stretch the definition.

My department chairman handed me a petition a few days after I arrived. I signed, one of thousands, he told me, who supported the Upper Peninsula as our fifty-first state. "The Wilderness State," he said. "The U.P."

U.P., D.C., UPI—I didn't give two shits as long as no one could find me.

"Without the bridge," he said, "we're not even connected to Michigan." He said his wife, all the wives who city-shopped, shopped in Green Bay. He said, "At least honor the land-mass—let us be part of Wisconsin!"

I agreed. It's my first year and I'll say almost anything because God knows I need the money. Fifteen hours of comp per week, 119 students, and my department chairman tells me I beat out applicants from twelve states, including a woman with a Ph.D. from Alaska. Jesus, I think, how abso-lutely depressing.

The good students have all tested out of the comp program, and I'm stuck with Weasel Conroy and his girlfriend Marcia Savage, a townie who says I'll get to love it here—the lakes and rivers *and* the snow. She says she does. She's ended her essay this way: *And so on and so forth.* They've got to be yanking my chain with names like Weasel and Savage, study-ing sentence structure in the Wilderness State.

Henry Gage, the short and unattractive class intellectual, said to me first day when I called the roll, "Call me Hank."

"Like in Hank Aaron," I said and smiled and he said back, "Like in who?"

I think, *C'mon, I don't need this right off the bat.* I've always taken an immediate and permanent dislike toward people, especially guys, who claim to know jack shit about baseball, and I used to tell them that, but I don't anymore. I let it pass like I do a lot of things.

I said to Henry Gage, "Hank it is." But when he wrote, camouflaged in the middle of a sentence on last week's assignment, *Check here if you've read this far,* I jotted him a note in the margin. *Surprise surprise,* I said. *Here's your check, Henry,* and I made a big one with a red pen, and then I wrote, *And this is as far as I go.* Then I printed his grade—F. I'd love to fail his ass for the whole semester, but the creep takes severe notes and reads everything I pass out and never misses a class, so it won't be easy. If, even for one minute, I ever really believed I'd father a kid like Henry Gage, I swear I'd cut my pecker off.

I'd give twenty-five—no, make that an even fifty percent—of my take-home pay to anyone competent and willing to correct these essays, anyone. I ask Charlie Waddell, my office mate and certain lifer, what he thinks and he says, "That's what we hired *you* for." So I carry the damn things home again in my briefcase and promise myself I'll read seventeen a day, seven days a week. The department chairman checks to make sure the students are writing and getting their papers back each week, getting their lousy money's worth. He's of the NO-FREE-TIME-ON-OUR-HANDS SCHOOL.

Still, I buy in, sort of. I tell my students they should care about language, and I mean it. Weasel says after class, "We care, or I do anyway," and Marcia nods and I think, maybe Charlie's right, maybe there is something that surfaces from all of this. Not writers, certainly, but something.

It's not my first teaching job, I remind Charlie at least once a day, but he's been here since 1970, and though he's only a few years older, he likes to lecture me, the new kid on the block. He says, "In Detroit you'd have to teach your classes wearing a bulletproof vest."

"Standard issue?" I ask him and he says, "Hey, that's no shit."

I lie. I say, "I survived two tours in Vietnam," which seems okay to say these days. "What's to fear?"

"You've got it good here, soldier," he says, but I don't look like a soldier in my civies—white shirt, open to the neck, thin tie, blue jeans. My M.A.'s from Yale and I've got Hopkins and

Stevens and Williams on my shelves. Charlie has said to me more than once, "There are no scholars in this bunch," and I can see he's proud of that. Nuts-and-bolts curriculum.

They all teach comp too, "Just like you do," Charlie says, "same as you." But I'm not one of them which is why I'm not well liked in this department of five men, a kind of sporting club. I lie to get a foothold, to keep an edge on these bone-heads who gather in my office for meetings because Charlie's got a miniature basketball hoop attached to the wall. They like the name of Minnesota's expansion team—The Timber-wolves. I tell them I played a little college hoop, another outrageous lie, and Charlie tosses me the Nerf ball and I step to the foul line they've chalked off behind his desk and, with-out ever taking a practice shot, I sink ten in a row. I'd love to get these candyasses on a real court, get Weasel, who I'm sure has never dribbled a B-ball, but who is lean and wiry and goes a good six-two, a leaper, to hustle down to the gym and the two of us would take off our shirts and we'd take on the four of them, all pot-bellied and tenured.

Charlie encourages me to encourage my students to enter essay contests around the country—religious, political, liter-ary. Instead I encourage them not to. *Play the lottery*, I want to tell them. *It's up to twelve million and all it takes is luck.*

But Charlie hands me yet another announcement in the hall between classes, a CALL FOR MANUSCRIPTS, and I stop right there and open my briefcase and say, "Take one, go on."

"Any one?" he asks and I say, "Read one and you've read them all," and he does take one from the middle of the stack and skims it and says he likes the simile, *a cloud like a giant nipple.*

"You've seen a nipple like that?" I ask him and he says, "If you think about it long enough," and I say, "Exactly," but as always he misses the point and walks away.

They love it here and it's more and more obvious every day that I don't, plus they know now that I taught creative writ-

ing at a university in Massachusetts for one year where almost nobody ice fishes, nobody I know. These guys spend
most of every weekend in their shanties out on the bay, fishing smelt.

"Make *that* exciting," I challenged my classes one day, and
Marian Montjoy did. She described, in great detail, how,
when she fished alone some nights in her father's hut, she'd
lock the door and take up the lines and stoke the stove until
she started to sweat. Then she'd take off all her clothes and
lower herself slowly through that hole into the icy water.
Nothing apocalyptic, and certainly no flow to the prose, but
she did hold my interest, so I gave her an A, the only one I'd
given all year, and asked her to drop around during my office
hours when I knew Charlie wouldn't be there. She did, and I
said, holding and pointing to her essay, "You don't really do
this," and she said, "No, no I don't," but she went on to say
how it resembled something else, how, during the big winter
storms, she runs naked from her sauna and dives headfirst
into the deepest drifts of snow. She's rich, this one. She's
trouble.

"That's okay, isn't it? I mean, to make it up?"

I tell her I've been making it up all my life, that and drinking too much and falling too quickly in love, and I say to
myself, *Uh-huh, don't do it*, but it's too late and I lean forward
far enough to let Marian Montjoy know the next move is hers.
I don't know, maybe subconsciously I want to get fired, get
out of here, though I have no place else in the world to go,
which is what I tell her later, and I admit I'm thirty-seven
and divorced, all this while sitting naked on the edge of my
bed. I don't feel badly though, not really, nor does she. She's
eighteen and still under the covers and she says, "Give me an
A for the course and I won't tell."

"No deal," I say, and she smiles and spends the night anyway and I drive her back to the edge of campus next morning
and don't hear from her again. I check at the registrar's office,
but she hasn't dropped the class. And I've heard nothing from

the dean. Maybe she'll spill the beans when I fail her, which I will, for unexcused absences, but so far not a peep.

You can't survive in a small town banging the co-eds. That's what my ex-wife said to me when I first started hanging around the college bars back in Massachusetts, drinking draft beer with my poetry workshop and bullshitting about curing the world with our poems. It sounded stupid even then, still in my twenties. *A young writer of promise,* as one reviewer of my first and only book once said about me. *Watch for him down the road,* and my wife did, literally, sitting alone on the couch in the dark of our rented efficiency, night after night, waiting for me to come home.

"Which one is it?" she asked one morning at breakfast and I said, still staring hungover into my plate, "Guess," and she did and got it right on the first try.

For once I didn't lie. I said, "Yes."

She said, "Do you love her?" and I answered honestly again. I said, "No, I do not," which felt good when I said it but then didn't seem to matter. After a short pause she said, "I'm moving out," but it was me who left, carrying a single suitcase. As I walked away toward the university, she shouted at me from the bedroom window, "Resign or I'll blow the fucking whistle, so help me God I will." Then she called me a whore but I didn't turn around, and she screamed that whores had no place in education, fucking these kids over.

Which I know now is true and, although I haven't changed much, Weasel Conroy says he's going to sign-up for every course I ever teach. I tell him he'll have to fail then and retake comp because it's all they'll give me. "Professor," he says, "I do like you, but I don't like nobody *that* much." I smile and Marcia says if they ever get married, which they will, they want me to read a poem of mine at the wedding, and they want to name their first son after me. "Sure," I say, "great," and Weasel slaps me on the back, right there in the Student Union lobby where I'm buying the local newspaper. And

Charlie Waddell, who has just gotten into the cafeteria line, gives thumbs-up while holding his tray. Even from this distance I can see his stack of essays is about the same as mine, some of them in those colored, see-through folders I tell my students never to use.

Weasel says, "How come when you teach us you always rock back and forth on your heels?"

"I don't, do I?"

"Yes," Marcia says, "you do, and you touch your upper lip a lot, like this, like someone with a mustache," and she shows me and of course I don't want to believe her, the way I don't want to believe that I'll grow to love the snow which, since leaving the Student Union, is coming down so hard everyone I pass is a blur.

In the middle of the quad the snow is almost blue in the half-light, blue like the color of smelt, the color of Marian Montjoy's eyes.

I drop my briefcase by my feet and I stand there, holding the collar of my sport coat as high as I can around my ears. I can make out my lighted office window, but I do not want to go inside, though I'm shaking now, and badly. I think, *The Wilderness State*—names like Weasel and Savage, lovers of rivers and Timberwolves, a place so cut-off that beautiful women throw themselves naked into the snow. I tell myself it's no fluke that we end up where we do, not kneeling at the hearth, but freezing and staring into the bluish night, and believing that moment *is* the moment when all the beasts we've ever been bow their heads and are rescued.

AUGUST SALES

August Sales is thirty-six, nine years older than me, and he's not that big. And although I've seen him in only one fight, I'm guessing he could lick most guys in the world. But it's not in him to do that. He says it's all those years of phenobarbital his mother gave him to stop the sleepwalking. I'm not so sure that's true—I don't think it is.

I know August well now, and I'm no doctor, but it seems to me the sleepwalking kicks in when the day has gone badly. Some nights he'll tell me, like he can feel it coming on, "Lock my bedroom door, Warren," which I do, with a key from the outside, and sure enough I'll hear the doorknob turning back and forth, back and forth, sometimes for hours. I opened it only one time, after he first moved in four years ago, and he was standing right in front of me and I said, "Hey, August, hey buddy," and I thought he heard me because his eyes were

· 7 5 ·

wide open like he'd seen a ghost. I tried to joke—I said, "Knock knock," and made like I was tapping on his forehead. He just stood there and I said, "Don't call me, I'll call you, right?" but not a word. Then he walked by me and outside to the porch stairs where he sat down in his underpants like it was summer. It wasn't cold for December, but it was cold to be outside like that and I thought, Jesus, and I said, "Hang on, August," as though he were somewhere I couldn't get him back from, on a cliff ledge or stuck down a well, and I ran into the house and grabbed my cigarettes and a blanket from the couch and a bottle of Jim Beam from the kitchen and two glasses and I sat next to him and poured us each a shot.

"Here," I said, and when he didn't take it, I closed his fingers around the glass and he held it without spilling a drop, even when I clinked the glasses and toasted him: "To you, August, goddamnit," and I belted one down and it warmed me in the chest. He didn't move and the whiskey in his glass looked smooth and coppery under the porch light. After a few silent minutes I stopped trying to see what August was seeing out there in the dark and I said, "Don't mind if I do," and I drank his shot too and then one more and, after draping the blanket over his shoulders, I said, "Good night," and left him there and went back to bed. I'd read somewhere that you should never wake a sleepwalker, that it's best to let them find their own way back. There must be something to that, because after maybe an hour I heard him come inside. I heard the back door shut, then his bedroom door. I slept soundly then and without dreams and when I awakened next morning, August was reading the newspaper at the kitchen table and drinking a cup of coffee.

He didn't remember a thing. "The two of us," I kept on. "I'm not bullshitting you, thirty-five frosty degrees and we're sitting side by side in our drawers. Jesus," I said, "no kidding, we're lucky nobody we know came by," and I laughed, losing it bad, and said how I was shivering my nuts off while he sat on the top stair, perfectly still, like he was posing for a goddamn photo. "Next time," I said, "I'm going to have the Polaroid ready."

Maybe I shouldn't have teased him beyond that, complimenting him on his perfect posture, "Like a schoolgirl's," I said, and I got up for more coffee and squeezed his shoulder on the way past to show it was all said in good fun. Then, remembering again how funny he looked, I said, "Out like a light, concentrating like you're on the pot," and I laughed harder, the way you do sometimes and can't stop until you look away, which I did, and out the window I could see the two deer in the pen, standing side by side but facing in opposite directions. When I turned around, August was staring up at me and he said, "Don't you ever open my bedroom door again, not ever." The fingers of both hands were splayed out on the table as though he might push himself up, the way I'd seen guys do late in the bars, slow and drunk and mad at the world and wanting a piece of someone real bad.

So I lowered my cup into the sink and closed my fists when he pushed his chair back. The muscles tightened in his forearms, but all he did was rub his eyes and he seemed exhausted then, as though he'd been beat up, and he pressed his forehead into his hands and I left him like that and went outside and into the polebarn.

Eight deer were hanging on hooks and, in the corner in the light, I noticed how the band saw's blade was pasty with tallow, the blade we used to cut rib chops. And, attached to a butcher's block, two meat grinders for hamburger and, stacked by the wall, lots of cardboard boxes from the A&P and rolls and rolls of freezer wrap. The phone kept ringing but I didn't answer it, and when anyone drove into the yard, a deer strapped to the top or the trunk of his car, I said August was under the weather and that I was behind with the processing and no way, nope, I couldn't take even one more.

Walt Kadrovach, who'd bow hunted some with August, said, "Where is he?" I said, "Asleep on the couch," and I pointed to the windows of the living room where I had tiptoed in and pulled the shades tight to the sills.

"He's hung over," Walt said and I said no he wasn't, that he had a stomach flu and Walt said, "Wake him." He said, "I don't care if he bends over and shits all the way to the dog pen, I got something I want the son-of-a-bitch to see. You too," he added, and hollered toward the house, "Sales, goddamnit," and then he opened his car door and I could see the cut-off head of an eight-point, a big spread, propped up on the front seat, its brown eyes open, its tongue crooked and pink in the sharp slant of the sunlight. When Walt reached in to blast the horn, I grabbed his arm.

"Leave him be," I said, and it came out much too harsh. I tried to soften it: "Listen, he's been out all night," I said, which in a crazy way *was* true, though misleading. When the hunting had been good, just last year, I had worked around the clock and did have to turn business away. But it hadn't snowed this deer season and the kill was low and, even though I was holding a knife and had bloodstains on my apron, Walt knew we weren't busy. He looked at my hand on his arm and I let it go and he got back in the car and took off his blaze-orange hat and hung it on one of the antlers. He'd stopped because he was excited and wanted to show off the rack to August and maybe make arrangements to get it mounted. I liked Walt, what little I knew of him, so I started the small talk. I asked, "Where'd you shoot him?" and Walt said back to me, "Up your ass," and I said, "Funny, I didn't feel or hear a thing."

I watched him drive away and I could see clouds moving in from the northwest and the temperature, at midday, was dropping fast. I had only one more hide to get off. More and more that was my job, skinning the deer out to help August keep up. Otherwise, I'd given the butchering part of the operation over to him, and it made a lot of money for us, all under the table, during those two weeks each year when the killing was good. I liked the other side of the business much better— the live deer part. I'd bought the first two over in Ishpeming, a buck and a doe, and I got a license from the state to breed them and to sell the meat. That was in the fall of 1980, two

years after an M-16 exploded in my hands and I lost most of
the little finger on my left hand, for which I was discharged
from the service and for which, each month for the rest of
my life, I'll receive a disability check in the mail. Nineteen
eighty, the year I tell people the yuppies turned from vegeta-
bles to venison and I signed contracts with three Chicago
restaurants. One of my buyers who hates the city told me I
satisfy the wilderness appetites of the rich. "They think it
improves their sex life," he said. And maybe it does. August
says not a chance, nothing would. He says he knows the type,
all dinks, but like I told him when he first joined me, money
talks. We keep the herd around twelve or fourteen now, cull-
ing it by one or two each month. Or rather, since I'm still
spooked by guns, I choose the deer and walk it into a separate pen and August squeezes the trigger. Some people, even
hunters, say how do you do it, and there's only one answer:
they're not pets.

August got spooked back then too, not by an exploding rifle,
but by his marriage, and he left his wife and his job as a
junior high school teacher and wrestling coach in Saginaw
and came north to the U.P. to work for the census bureau.
Which is how I met him, when he stopped by here and we
ended up shooting the breeze for over an hour, those first two
deer eating corn right from our hands.
  A few weeks later I sat with him in the bar. It was early and
he was half shit-faced and he said, "You knock on enough
doors, you'll knock on the wrong door, guaranteed." He said,
just that morning, he'd asked a man named Herb Vandenakker, a guy probably sixty, it was hard to tell, how many
residents in the house and Herb had said two, him and his
wife. And how many dogs, and Herb, tight-jawed, said none,
he didn't have any. But there was a lot of yapping and howl-
ing out back, August said, like there was a whole pack of
dogs, and he said he asked about that and Herb said, fuck it,
just fuck it all, and he slammed the door. August leaned
closer to me then and said, "Listen, I'm standing on this

slanted porch, writing myself a note on the form on my clipboard when I hear shots, one after the other every couple seconds, and the dogs are whining now, high pitched, and then there's nothing, not a sound, and I don't want to walk back to the car or even move. But I do, a couple of careful steps, and there's Herb Vandenakker at the corner of the house, and in the sun I can see the gray stubble of his beard and the size of his gut and he's got the fucking rifle in one hand but it's pointed at the ground thank God, and he's not dragging a beagle, he's holding it up by the scruff of its neck like some monstrosity of a rabbit he's shot, brown and black and white and it's wearing a collar. He holds it up for me to see how dead it is. 'Easy,' I tell him, 'easy now,' and he says he ain't got any dogs and I nod so he knows I believe him now, and I repeat just that, no dogs, and I write an exaggerated 0 in the appropriate box, and when I hold it out to him I notice, for the first time, there's a woman staring out the window and her face is not in her hands, her hands are not even visible. But her eyes are. And she's not staring at me or at the dog or at her husband. She's staring at nothing, because this thing that's happened has happened forever and blaming someone won't do any good. She's just there, a part of it and not part of it, this man's wife, this man who is crying now and has dropped to his knees and is hugging the dog and all because, one afternoon under a very blue sky, for a few lousy minutes, I entered his life.'"

"Christ," I said. "Jesus Christ, who'd you tell?" meaning the sheriff's department or someone higher up than August at the census or even the humane society, someone who could follow up, and August said, "I called my wife."

"Your wife? Why?" I asked, "What for?" and he said he didn't really know and that she told him he should count his lucky stars that he wasn't killed too, and that most likely the guy was a nut, a Vietnam vet, and that she was seeing a man now and that August shouldn't call her anymore. "What if I had died?" he'd asked her and she said, "Then you'd be dead," and she didn't hang up and neither did he, but nothing else was said for maybe five minutes, which he said might not sound like much, but that long distance it was an eternity. And in that silence August said he just kept seeing Herb Vandenakker's wife like a ghost behind the wavy glass, a person not really alive, an apparition about to float into the emptiness which is, he said, where all shock takes us, forever and alone.

He drank heavy for the rest of the night, tequilla and beers, and when he passed out I got some help putting him in the bed of the pickup, flat on his back, his arms out to the sides and, under the dim floodlights of the parking lot, he looked like a guy who'd fallen from a high roof, perhaps someone who'd just that day been counted by the census and now was dead, which meant the number of people alive in the county would be off at least by one, and I figured that must happen all the time in a world of guns and no guns, of accidents and sickness and old age and sadness. My father was dead and my mother, half-crazy with grief, had remarried immediately and was living with a man I'd never met, though they were still in Michigan last I heard and had invited me, when I was still in the army, to visit them anytime. August's father was dead too, a man, I'd later learn, who named his only son for the month the family farm went belly-up and was sold at auction.

I didn't know then where August lived, so I drove real slow over the bumpy roads toward my place. The sky was thick with stars and I wanted the ride to last, and I thought how the stars had been dying out for millions of years, which made our lives seem pretty small and temporary and unhappy like they got sometimes for everyone. And up ahead, blinded by the high beams, a doe and two fawns stood in the middle of the road. I killed the engine and put the truck in neutral and coasted down the gradual decline, seeing how close I could get, the doe's head jerking side to side, trying to see into the darkness behind the lights, trying to figure which way to run. I stopped, not twenty feet from them and turned off the headlights and sat there for a couple of minutes. I

heard August snoring in the truck bed and then the deer
crashing through the underbrush down the embankment. I
lit a cigarette and then I held the lighter close to my face and
twisted the rearview mirror so I could see my eyes which
were blue but in that small flame were no color, only glassy.
They were closing a little too, and I thought, if I leaned my
head back, I'd fall asleep right there, not a mile from home,
my drunk friend out cold in the back, and the moon, almost
full, directly above us. And I thought about Ellen Bogart
who'd been in the bar and who August agreed *was* pretty
but said she didn't belong to the Mid-American-Council-for-
Better-Virgins, and he said don't laugh, that he knew these
things, knew from the census that she was divorced with two
kids and living with a maniac named Billy Pascoe who'd
yelled from inside the house for Ellen to shut the hell up and
then he came outside and told August to scratch his name off
the goddamn form, that he wasn't permanent and that he
was touchy anyway about people nosing around, asking a lot
of questions. The name meant nothing to me, not then it
didn't. Herb Vandenakker, Billy Pascoe, Ellen Bogart, August
Sales, names to approximate the population of the counties,
and maybe change, every decade, the numbers on the signs
on the outskirts of each U.P. town so that people passing
through would know that much about our lives, that there
were 1,223 people here or 180 there or 74 farther north in the
town where the windows were mostly boarded and that single gas station with the flying red horse painted on front
had only one pump and it might be for kerosene for the
lamps. I thought then of Big Bay and Iron River and Ke-
weenaw, places I'd hung around a short time after getting out
of the service, before I bought the house and settled here. I
didn't have my name on the mailbox for over a year, but once
the business caught on, I painted, in red letters, Warren Lep-
pala, and after August moved in with me, I painted his name
there too.

Right after that his divorce papers came and I remember
how he skimmed the legal jargon, but stared a long time at

the line where he was supposed to sign his name. Finally he asked me for a pen and he did sign but he stared at the signature too, like he wasn't all that sure it was his. I watched him fold the papers and stuff them into an envelope and seal it and walk, without his coat, outside into the cold. He waited a while before sliding the envelope into the mailbox. Then he raised the red metal flag and looked both ways, up and down the dirt road, as though expecting somebody he knew to drive by. His breath kept rising in quick white bursts, like he'd been running, and he stood there until I stepped out and called to him. "Come on back, August," I said, and he did.

Next morning he waited by the kitchen window for Art Casey, the mail carrier, who reached from his car and took the envelope and, left off, rubberbanded together, some catalogs and my disability check and a letter for August from his wife. He read it in his bedroom, the door open, and from where I was sitting on the couch, I could see him look up every few seconds from the letter, as if every word was emblazoned, as if she were explaining things perfectly for the first time, things he hadn't ever understood before, good things, I hoped, like how she knew they'd used up all their second chances, but believed deep down that they'd both realize, somewhere down the road, that parts of it *had* been right and important and that those parts would always break their hearts. I'd like to believe that's what she said, but I don't think she did. That night, before bed, was the first time August ever mentioned his sleepwalking and I locked his door and put the key on my dresser and, as I shouldn't have, opened the door and teased him that one time. I think it contributed to what happened next on the landing of Mc-Cauley's Feed and Grain.

It had stayed cold and we were there to pick up some irrigation hose and shucked corn and I could tell August recognized the new guy who was yelling, "C'mon, c'mon, you got another foot," as August backed the pickup, tailgate down, tight to the loading platform. Out the sideview mirror I could see the guy reading over the order sheet, lifting the bill of his cap and scratching along his hairline with his thumb, like he didn't quite know where certain things were yet. Me and August could have sat in the cab, staying warm and smoking cigarettes, but the snow was swirling so we pulled on our gloves and got out to help him.

Right off the guy says to August, "I know you, where do I know you from?"

"No place," August said, and he started into the warehouse.

"Whoa," the guy said, "slow down." Then he took a couple of steps toward August and he said, "Where's the sign says you walk in here and help yourself? I mean, shit, I ain't standing here in the fucking snow for my health, do you suppose?"

August turned around and all he said was, "Good, that's fine," and he started back toward the truck and the guy, kind of twisting his head this way and that for a better angle, said again, "I know you, I know this whole act," and then he remembered. "The fucking census," he said, "you're that exterminator."

"Enumerator," August said, "I counted people and dogs, not cockroaches."

"Uh-uh," the guy said, "no sir, it ain't numbers, it's names," and August said to me, "Meet Billy Pascoe," and Billy said to August, "Hey, how come you remember my name so good?"

"I went to college," August said, which was true, of course, down to U of Michigan, but it was the way he said it. I tried to head the trouble off, but after I said what I did, it sounded stupid—I said, "It's cold out here," and Billy Pascoe didn't even look at me. Instead, he explained how he'd asked around about August, but he didn't call him that, he called him Soupy, Soupy Sales. People like August don't like to be teased that way, not when their name is such a sad occasion. So, when Billy said it a second time, August hit him, one solid right hand flush on the bridge of the nose, and Billy dropped hard and I could see he was going to try and get up but that he couldn't. All he could do was move a couple of inches at a time on his forehead and knees, leaving a dark streak of blood in the snow. It happened that fast and was over.

We heard, after a few days, that Billy Pascoe had threatened around town that he'd see August dead. And maybe that's what he meant to do because, when he was stopped in a stolen car, he was headed this way, a loaded pistol under the front seat. We read in the newspaper later that he'd been linked to an armed robbery downstate and was being held without bail. I cut the article out, but August crumpled it up and threw it away. "Fuck him," he said. Then he said, "Let's get out of the house, let's go see a movie." I said no, but that after I fed the deer I'd drive with him into town and wait for him at the bar until the show let out.

I knew it was crazy, but Ellen Bogart was alone in a booth in back and I walked over after a while and sat down and bought her a drink. I hadn't felt like getting drunk, so I'd been drinking quinine water and lime, a drink my father used to make, though I wasn't thinking about him when I ordered it. I was just tired of winter and the quinine sounded summery. And there was Ellen Bogart wearing a sleeveless, flowered dress. I could see the edge of her slip strap on her shoulder, and she wasn't nearly so pretty close up, but I liked the way she held her cigarette and pressed her thumb to her cheekbone, like an actress, and I asked her if she was any relation to Humphrey Bogart and she smiled like she'd been asked that a million times.

"Maybe," she said, but later in the conversation she mentioned her trailer house and how the pipes had frozen twice and that one of her kids had been sick and how, sometimes on a still night, while shoveling snow from her roof, it would dawn on her that this *was* her life, as far as she was headed toward stardom.

"You never know," I said, "crazier things happen."

"This far off in the boonies?" she asked and I said, "Why

not?" which wasn't really a question, and she shrugged and I told her how I had meant, a bunch of times one other night, to buy her a drink.

"Too shy?" she asked and I said, "No, bad advice from a friend who told me not to do it."

"A woman friend?"

"No," I said again, "A guy going through a tough divorce," and I hated the way that sounded.

"I've been there," she said. And a lot further, I thought, but I didn't want to know right then where that was, so I looked at my watch and stood up, and when I did she touched my hand, the one with the missing finger. "An old war wound," I said and she shook her head no. She said, "You're too young for that," and I bent over and kissed her softly on her mouth.

"I hate you men," she said, but she pulled me to her and this time she put both her hands behind my head and kissed me hard. "Like Hollywood," she said, and that phrase stayed in my head as I leaned against the old brick under the blinking lights of the marquee, smoking and waiting for August.

When the show finally let out, some John Wayne remake, only a few people came through the doors. I looked in, and then I knocked on the glass pane, and just as the usher let me in, August walked slowly into the lobby, looking a lot like a sleepwalker. But this time he was wide awake and he said to me, getting into the truck, "Lock my door tonight," and I said, "Let's not go to bed," and I took the map from the glove compartment and I said, "Where to?" He turned the key in the ignition and shifted into first and he said, "Anywhere's good," and, when he let off the clutch, I knew we'd get safely back home, but not until after first light.

DEVOTION

Men always described her as a woman with perfect teeth. It was the first thing, meeting her, that they commented about—even educated men, her department chairman during an interview, for example—how sparkly white and straight they were, and how it was easy to visualize her doing Ultra-Bright or Colgate commercials. Sometimes she was even asked if she had. No, she'd say, smiling and flattered but anxious also to change the subject. A pretty face, she thought, simply was not that important.

Until last week it wasn't. Until February 10, to be exact, when, unable finally to chew even soft foods, she'd had all thirty-two teeth extracted. One for each year of her life, she thought, though whenever she stared into the bathroom mirror now, she appeared more than twice that old, her face misshapen and splotchy and almost unrecognizable. In that harsh light she'd flash back to the article she'd read in the hospital in *People* magazine, about women injecting their lips with silicon to make them full and seductive—like Madonna's, it said. She'd wonder what Madonna would look like tight-lipped, without teeth, dancing and singing "Justify My Love," and whether any man would watch the video and still fantasize about kissing her. She guessed not, feeling the long curves of black stitches inside her mouth with the tip of her tongue.

For months before she agreed to the operation, she had lived not in "discomfort," as her dentist had predicted, but more often in agony, her headaches incessant and severe. There was no cure for what he called simply, "brittle teeth," inherited, she knew, from her father's side of the family. She had lost weight, and one morning a student of hers—an odd and tall and skinny young woman whom she liked—paused in midsentence and then, staring at her, asked point-blank, "Are you bulimic too?" As soon as the student had gone, she closed her office door and turned slowly around, leaning against it, her face in her hands. After a few minutes she telephoned the oral surgeon's office and said, right before she burst out crying, that she had pretended long enough, that she hurt something awful every, every day. Then she uttered the unspeakable—she said, "Yes," it was past time, she had to have them out.

Followed by the practical questions: How soon and what portion of the cost would Blue Cross cover? How many nights in the hospital? Would she be able then to drive herself home? Before leaving that afternoon from school, she typed up a request for an emergency leave from the university to begin at semester's end, less than a month away. To her colleagues who asked, she said simply that she needed the time—which wasn't a lie. She was using it now to sit up alone nights and heal. No matter where she set the thermostat, she still felt cold, so she had moved her chair back a ways from the window, closer to the space heater she'd turned up to high. In the directness of that coiled orange heat, sometimes she'd fall asleep.

And dream or no dream, she would awaken to snow swirling outside or, on clear, subzero nights like this one with the moon almost full, to the view of Ice Town in the distance—bleached and haunted, but beautiful too—illuminated like an Ansel Adams photograph. Ice Town was the name the locals had given to the village of shanties (she'd once counted over two hundred of them) clustered in small colonies on the Bay. Though she had lived in northern Michigan for almost seven years, she had never been inside a shanty. Ice fishing seemed to her, an assistant professor of psychology, absolutely the most cretinous of all earthly activities. That was unfair, and she knew it. She could only imagine the kind of men who hunkered down inside those huts—forklift operators from Red Mill, the lumberyard outside of town, or handymen you could call up for minor plumbing or carpentry repairs or, this ghostly time of year, to get your roof shoveled after a storm. These, she imagined, were the men who left before dawn for home, half-drunk fishermen carrying pails of smelt to be cleaned by their wives.

She worried, whenever one of them would ride his snowmobile across the ice and up the frozen boat ramp and onto her street, that he would slow down by her house, the only one on the hill, and turn around and cruise by another time or two before killing his headlight and pulling into her driveway. Then, she imagined, he'd steer right into the carport behind her Mustang, where he'd unstrap his black helmet and take it off and just sit there, drinking peppermint schnapps and smoking a cigarette below the steamy bathroom window, waiting.

And that's the reason she still had the pistol and always kept it near her, a .32 caliber Beretta—what her ex-husband, loading the clip, had at first called a "home-protection weapon." But as he played poker late one Friday night with his buddies—she in earshot, correcting midterms in the next room—he had referred to it as a "snub-nose," as though it were designed specifically to fire close range into somebody's face. He said every "squeeze," meaning girlfriend or wife, should own one, especially in the goddamn boonies. She hated the crude way he sometimes talked around men, usually after a few beers or some dope, saying that all a guy needed when he was depressed or bored was a decent knob-job, a hummer. She guessed he had probably gotten a few from the coeds she knew he met in the bars—literary groupies—but she asked no questions. He had high cheekbones and shiny black hair and had published a successful first novel that was still widely read on campus, all reasons why she had followed him so far north and married him and agreed, in a brief ceremony, to love, honor, and ignore, meaning they agreed not to hound each other, not to ask a lot of petty and jealous questions. His name was Doy Hunt, her name Sheila Knight. That was the big joke after their divorce, that they were like Knight and Doy, so perfectly mismatched.

Sheila had neither wanted nor not wanted a handgun back then—she'd let Doy, the cowboy from Montana with fierce dark eyes, deal with intruders. But before finally moving out on her for good, he'd insisted she keep it, inventing gruesome scenarios of women being raped and murdered and buried in their own basements, each razory detail like something right out of *Helter Skelter*. He had the gun with him in his truck, a Powerwagon, the last time he picked her up after her classes. All year he'd been on sabbatical, working mornings on a new book. It was winter then too, and there in faculty parking, the engine idling, he showed her how to click the safety off with her thumb, and how to hold the piece (that's what he was calling it by then) with two hands, "Out in front of your face," he said. He said, "Like this," and through the windshield, his arms steady, he took careful aim on an older woman Sheila did not know by name, though they had greeted each other with a nod in the blowing snow of a blizzard once, both of them leaning into the wind on their way toward the psychology and religion building, briefcases shielding their faces.

"And you squeeze," he said. "That's the secret. You never *ever* jerk the trigger and you never talk and you don't let him talk. You squeeze and then you do it again and again until you've emptied every round into the miserable scuzbag." He reached over and lightly touched her shoulder, then behind her ear with the back of his fingers. He said, "Take it. Take the fucking gun, Sheila." He was holding it out to her by the short steel-blue barrel with his other hand, and she did take it. It felt lighter than she'd expected, which was all she could think to say to him, and he said back, "That's good, that's perfect." He punched in the lighter and waited, staring at it until it popped. He lit the cigarette and cracked the vent window and, shifting into first gear, he told her he'd sleep better now. So she asked him—for the first time—"In who's bed?" and to her surprise he'd actually given her a name: a woman back East, he said, in Massachusetts, where he'd given a reading that fall and had been offered a job, right on the spot, as a resident writer in a small private college in Boston—a city, Sheila had always believed, where she would like to be.

There had been nights during their marriage when he did not come home—not a lot of nights, but some, and always in the summer when he'd leave his desk, as he put it, to recharge and go nuts. The first time it happened she stayed up reading and sipping wine and waiting, nauseous with worry. He arrived just after first light and knocked tentatively on the front door—knocked, she believed back then, to see if she'd let him in. He was soaking wet and smiling like a little kid, and he held up a jar half filled with water, clear like cold tap water. And inside, a lamprey. She remembered how relieved she'd been, and how, blocking the entrance, her hands pressing the doorjamb, she said to him, "*You*, okay. *It* stays outside!"

But it didn't for long, ending up that afternoon in the aquarium, with its fleshy round hole of a mouth suctioned to the glass. For maybe a week it stayed that way, its tail wavering slowly back and forth. Then one morning, when Sheila lifted the lid to feed the goldfish, all four were dead and white and floating upside down above the bluish-green gravel, the filter humming. The lamprey was in the same exact spot on the glass and Sheila, while Doy was still in the shower, reached into the tank with a pair of long-bladed scissors and cut the eel in half. She had expected, as with a worm or a spaded snake, that the two halves would twist in violent loops and spasms, thin-threaded clouds of blood drifting to the surface. That didn't happen and, stooped over, she stared close-up into that dark mouth as though she might be able to see right through it. What she saw instead was its pink throat opening and closing, and she reached in again and this time severed it right behind the head, whispering, "Die, die," with the lamprey the whole time just eye-balling her as if nothing had happened. Nothing at all.

And that's what Doy saw when he walked naked into the bedroom, just that mottled brown head sucking the glass and his wife pointing at it with the closed tip of the scissors and breathing hard. Doy's hair was slicked back and, pretending to shiver, he pressed his knees together and covered his dick with both hands and said, "Remind me never to piss you off." They both laughed wildly, making furious love a few minutes later sideways on the bed. Sheila frenched Doy deeper than she ever had, and then it was *his* tongue swimming in *her* mouth, across her perfect teeth, the two of them grunting and, for once, coming together at the same time.

What he had said years later, right before driving out of the parking lot, was not so funny. He'd said to Sheila, "Listen, life's a bummer sometimes, babe," and that one sentence, so banal, seemed the cruelest thing he'd ever said to her. She had wanted to tell him he had a real way with words, but she was no good at sarcasm. She responded instead by nodding and closing her eyes awhile and, on the ride home, she tried hard not to think about being single and afraid, something she had never considered seriously before in her adult life. She also tried not to think about the children she wanted badly and would never have by him, nor about the house they had bought together—broken dumbwaiter and faulty wiring and all—a renovation project that was suddenly in her name alone. No, she tried to think instead about herself as a killer, and she carefully placed the loaded gun on top of the stack of freshman essays on her lap—all on the topic of "Men and Marriage in the 80s." It was laughable, but she had no sense of humor that day, thinking, as Doy turned on the headlights and wipers and slowed for a sudden squall on the back road between the blueberry bogs, that it would be one sorry goddamn son of a bitch who ever broke in and came toward her.

It was a kid who was about to, maybe eighteen or nineteen years old, and he was not some imagined rough customer from Ice Town, but a student from the university. For hours Sheila's mind had been jumping from one thing to another— crazy things like the feel of a clarinet reed on her tongue, how she had loved the instrument but given it up when her mother convinced her it would make her bucktoothed and ugly. And how her father had had a name for the embarrass- ing image on his forearm—a "titty tattoo," a faded blue outline that even a skin graft could not remove. "We make mistakes," is what he'd told her that day she asked him never to wear short sleeves. Mistakes. And here she was regretting that she had not answered Doy's letters, asking how she was. And just that quickly the image was of him again, smoking a joint at the kitchen table one evening before dinner. He'd gotten angrier and angrier, she remembered, at a woman editor in New York who'd rejected his latest short story, calling his work "dangerous." The note paperclipped to the story said that the editor's *intuition* told her not to touch this one. "Intuit this," Doy had finally said, leaning back in his chair and grabbing his crotch. "Dangerous. Christ almighty, women don't know dangerous. Their instincts are fucking all tapped out!"

But Sheila, even half-asleep, wearing a nightgown and a shawl around her shoulders and thick wool socks, sensed that a prowler was outside well before she heard him kicking at the rolled and frozen newspapers on the front stoop. At first she thought that was all he was after, the want ads perhaps, someone laid off and shamed in the middle of this particular winter night into looking for work. It could happen. She knew about freaky human behavior and more than a little about shame—she felt it deeply each time she mashed up bananas and canned tangerines and pear slices in the blender: like pabulum, she thought, like baby food—except for the shot of rum.

What if it was Francine? Not a good friend certainly (she hadn't made any of those), but someone who might check up, noticing that the driveway had gone unplowed, that there had been no lights on in the house for almost a week. Sheila could not face anyone she knew, nor could she talk very long without pain, which is why she had unplugged the phone. Her hair was uncombed and it would be another two days before she was to be fitted for dentures—before, as she saw it, she got her lips back so that she could once again enunciate. If anybody knocked, she would not go to the door. For several minutes there was no sound except the distant ringing she sometimes heard during certain long silences, deep inside her ears. Then, almost startling her, the refrigerator kicked on and there was the sudden cold tapping of wind chimes from the backyard.

Which was when she saw him, leaning out from the porch, craning to see in the window, one hand holding onto the railing, the other out in front of his face as though he were waving to her, as though the window would begin soon to move away like the window of a train. But she was traveling nowhere, a sick frail woman who was right then reaching down by her feet for a gun. When she looked back, the man had vanished, and for that moment she was almost certain she had hallucinated, the way she'd done lately, exhausted and drinking rum along with her 500-milligram doses of erythromycin. Doy, after writing all day, would do much worse things to his body—Quaaludes and grass and Old

Museum bourbon—but never while handling a pistol, and Sheila might have put it back on the floor if a gloved fist had not smashed through one of the narrow wavy panes that bordered the front door, the slivers of glass splashing phosphorescent into a pool of moonlight.

That was all she had to see by, and she watched the hand feel for the lock and snap it up and then the doorknob turning and the door opening and closing behind him, a cold draft already seeping in, and him just standing there, not ten feet away in the grainy semidarkness. He unzipped his parka and reached into his shirt pocket. What Sheila heard next was that little pop the cap makes when snapped off a tube of Chap Stick, and she watched calmly as he circled his mouth, first one way and then back the other.

What wasn't clear in her mind was whether she would shoot him or not if he tried to flee when she reached slowly over and switched on the lamp. Which she did finally, while he was on his knees, rummaging through the hall closet. She knew him immediately, even with the knit cap pulled low over his forehead, and she knew also, in the short silence that followed, that he did not recognize her, though he had stared at her from his back-row seat more intently than any student she had ever had in a class. He had never once participated, but he talked when he noticed the gun. He said, "Please, lady." He said, "Please, I swear to God I didn't know anybody was here. Please." And he stood and slid the two pairs of ice skates from his shoulder and held them out to her by the laces, her white figure skates and Doy's unused black ones. "I just wanted to get warm," he said. "I didn't mean to steal anything, holy shit."

She paused a long minute and then she mumbled, "Put them on," and he understood her. Without asking why, he said, "Okay, sure," and nodded at her and sat down on the hardwood floor and pulled off his boots and did what she had said.

"Now mine," she said when he'd finished, and he slid forward on his rear end, slid up close to her, and she thought,

"Snub-nose," as she raised it to his face, the safety off. He flinched, but then carefully took each of her feet, she lifting to help. While he laced, she thought about how students sometimes fell madly in love with their teachers rather than with knowledge, and how Doy had most likely crossed that line, screwing them and surviving it, getting offered and accepting new jobs where the women would always be young and rich and beautiful and much too easily seduced. Not nearly the crime she was now committing at gunpoint, of course, forcing this boy outside onto the porch, the two of them walking wobbly on the tips of the blades, the snow glittering and the stars as bright as she'd ever seen them, the constellations throbbing in the sky above Ice Town and this intruder still pleading, "Please, I'm sorry," and trembling badly—certain, Sheila believed, that she was crazy enough to shoot him if he did not lean down to kiss her. So when she brought her mouth toward his, he did, his hands still clasped, as she had instructed him to do, behind his back—like a lover, she thought, gliding toward her across the clear ice of a pond. And she almost asked him to hug her now that she had started to shiver. But he'd been punished enough, so she said to him, and it was not more than a whisper, "Go then." And he left, still wearing her ex-husband's skates and running furiously through deep snow away from that tiny rink of porch, stumbling several times, falling once face-first at the far edge of her yard by the woods. And when she lost sight of him she could actually see his shadow moving diagonally through the long white spaces between the trees, downhill in the direction of the shanties.

She was breathing hard, her lungs aching from the cold air, the warm vapor crystallizing on her cheeks—all signs of frostbite, with the thermometer at fifteen below. But she stayed outside another minute, staring down over the Bay, a woman wearing only a nightgown, a shawl like a scarf, and white ice skates with blue pompoms. And thinking clearly now how people were sometimes not themselves, and that forgiving them had always been her devotion.

FUGITIVE

What you need to remember is that my name is Raymond
Keeway and that I do not know how to hot-wire a car, but
that I did steal one from the Detroit Metro parking lot on July
1st, late in the afternoon, when I flew home without any
luggage from St. Paul where I'd been for less than four hours,
trying to patch things up with a woman. Coming out of the
terminal I flagged down a cab, but when he pulled over I said
to myself, screw it, screw it all, and walked quickly away.

If questioned now, I would say the theft was not premedi-
tated. All I remember is trying a lot of doors before I found
one open, keys under the floor mat, and I got in and started
the car, a shiny black BMW with tinted glass, which I guess
made this grand larceny but didn't bother me because I
believe there comes a time when a guy snaps and crimes of
madness don't matter anymore. My father, who served some

hard time when I was a kid, warned me, before he left for prison at Jackson, that crime was a habit, like gambling or cigarettes, and contagious in a family so that you could refer to names like Stambaugh or Bausch or Gottwalled as good-for-nothings, which included even the little children, the miniatures, he called them, and nobody can convince me now that he was wrong.

There was no pistol in the glove compartment or under the seat, so I can tell you, and you can believe me because I don't lie, that on my way north that night into the U.P., I did not knock off a fireworks stand or a Shell mini-mart, and I did not stop for the leggy young hitchhiker in nylons and high heels who licked her lips and smiled at me on the outskirts of Naubinway at dusk when I was already tired and, at gun-point, force her into the cramped trunk of the car, though none of those things seems farfetched to me.

Maybe it will surprise you to hear I attended Catholic schools and that it was there I learned that my father was blaspheming at home whenever he said, "Jumping Jesus Christ," which he did often and I thought was funny and always laughed, and that it was one of the nuns, the good sister Theresa, who took me aside after school, right after my father had been arrested for the second time for badly beating up another man, and she said, calling me "Hon," "Kneel with me," and I got down on the hard dark tiles beside her desk and closed my eyes and she promised me I'd be spared my father's sins, but we all know that there are things in this world, real bad things, that she could never in a million years have comprehended.

She was old then and I imagine that she, like my mother and my father, is dead. I am thirty-nine and have no kids, though that is unintentional because I was married once and wanted a family, a boy and a girl, so I could stand on the sledpath, watching them in their bright red snowsuits, glide toward me down the big hill behind our house. Back then I made love with my wife at least once a night, and never any birth control. I realized, fifteen years later, that fatherhood is bordering on pure fantasy, especially since I get aroused so infrequently these days (ask the woman in St. Paul), so you can figure there's little danger of rape in this story. But believe me, I don't rule out the extraordinary taking place, like me pulling into a bar in Iron River or Gibbs City and leaving after closing time with the only waitress there and driving toward her place with the moon-roof open and the Patsy Cline tape she's handed me from her pocketbook playing on the car stereo, her seat reclined all the way so she can stare up at the arrangement of stars. Let's say there's an extra button open on her blouse and the wind is blowing her dark hair back from her forehead. Maybe that's when I decide to slow down and, without warning, pull off of old Route 9. That's the moment, isn't it, when something awful could begin to happen at the edge of the newly disked field. She could get suddenly scared and start to cry and jump out of the car, panicked and yelling, "Help, somebody please help me!" and I'd have to tackle her hard and turn her over on her back, holding both her wrists tightly to the ground, the whole weight of my body struggling and struggling on top of her, trying to calm her down. Yes, I'm convinced these things can happen and do and that it's the misfortune of people like her, the victims of unhappiness who surrender, for even a little while, to the temptations of love, and always pay dearly.

And that's why, about the time I might pick up a woman, I usually lose my nerve, knowing how wrong one-nighters can go. Yet I've had women ask me if romance shouldn't be at least a little bit dangerous and I never hesitate to answer *No*. The woman in St. Paul accused me of always playing it safe, which she said is "boring, Raymond, boring, boring, boring," and, ultimately, in a relationship (a word I hate), a symptom of failure. "Loosen up," she said this last time she dumped me. She said, "Raymond, do yourself a big favor and quit that job at the bank and, just once in your lifetime, get rid of those hundred dollar shoes and that blue suit and go get yourself in some serious trouble." So I stole the BMW and headed north where I'd heard there was no law and, if my father was right and there is catharsis in crime, though he never used these words, where I might actually harm someone and not get caught and start to feel good again, and that's the part that always frightens me so goddamn much.

I'm not making this up. Listen, I read a story once about this guy in Florida, no previous record, never an arrest or even a parking violation, no loitering on the corner in front of Sardies or Hampton News or whatever hangout, who, after going on a shooting spree in a mall one Sunday at noon, placed the shotgun barrel under his chin and, before squeezing the trigger, smiled and said to all those people cowering behind the water fountain and under the benches, their hands over their ears, "Resist nothing, resist no urge."

There, more free advice, and it's not easy to dismiss, coming from a man whose neighbors said acted perfectly sane, a man with a family and friends and a badminton net and a gas grill in his backyard. You say we deserve better council, and I agree absolutely, but I can't help thinking that there was a warning there, a profound psychological truth, *before* the final and desperate end.

Sure, we've heard a thousand shockers, like the third grade teacher knifed right in the classroom by her boyfriend, right under the tip of the American flag, and somebody says, "Yeah, but that's Detroit," but I don't laugh, and some other smart-ass pipes up, "Which might explain the fucking motive at least," but they don't remember that there was a boy in the back row sound asleep, his head on his desk, and he'd already repeated the third grade twice, the only student who wasn't paying attention, who wasn't a witness, and what was he, eleven years old? And he's the one who told the police that his classmates were wrong, dead wrong, that he'd seen his father do it and do it often, almost every night, but that it only happened in his dreams. *Right*, the cops must have said. *Okay, sure*, and there's no question the kid was a little slow in school and mixed up, but I don't agree that his version was completely wrong, the real and the unreal overlapping. But

I'll bet my life that the shrinks who were called in and set up office for the rest of the school year had a field day with him, predicting he'd drop out of school by fifteen and, from a distance, follow the attractive young female teachers home, follow them until they shut and locked their doors. Which, of course, even if they'd had dead bolts installed, is never enough protection against someone who wants badly enough to break in. I've often resisted that urge myself when I've been drunk on bourbon and cruising the neighborhoods, parking sometimes late at night across the street from my ex-wife's apartment, hating her for cleaning me out, financially and emotionally, during those long slow months of our divorce. And, like I said, I'm next to celibate now, but I'll admit there's something erotic in anger and I'm not convinced that the moans of sex don't ease from us all the pain inflicted over the years by those we've loved. Here's a simpler but cruder way to say it: muff, snatch, mound, the words I've heard men use, that breed I call low-life who always mean to fuck the world and to pull out feeling better.

I pushed on all night and stopped rarely and then only to pee in the dark. I don't remember what time I parked the car, almost out of gas, and walked barefoot and hungry on the beach at Ontonagon, the wind blowing west across Superior. But I do remember, at the water's edge at first light, staring at a pay phone some vandal must have ripped and thrown from the bridge. I could hear, with each wave, the coins inside and I thought then about certain long-distance calls I'd made in my life, you know the kind, not dialed from Texas or Idaho or North Dakota or even from overseas in the service, but rather from some imprecise yet permanent ache in the heart. And that's when I got scared and started running for the car and, out of breath, drove at one hundred miles an hour toward home until the needle descended below empty, and then I coasted, slower and slower to a stop on the long flat straightaway. I suppose I could have pushed the car, in neutral, down the embankment into the high grass, but I didn't do that. Call it weariness or surrender, but I just sat there, the emergency flashers pulsing, and I rolled down the window and lit a Lucky Strike, though I hadn't smoked a cigarette in years, and then another from the pack left on the seat, and I was sure a wolf or a bear would cross in front of me any second, and if one did, I promised myself I'd get out and follow a ways simply to test the wildness of this place where I'd arrived.

But that didn't happen. Instead, a transport trailer slowed coming the other way, its air brakes screeching, and when I yelled up to him, "Forget the car," and climbed into the huge cab, he said, "Here, wear this," and he handed me a Tigers baseball cap as though I needed a disguise, as though I were not some petty first offender out for an all-night joy ride, but rather someone hardcore, someone more like my father who promised it would be like this, my father who was profiled and considered "very dangerous" by the FBI and died of a heart attack at forty-five in a federal penitentiary.

"You're a fugitive," he said, and I thought of that old TV program, David Janssen fleeing each week into the dark and unresolved conclusion of every episode. "Yes," I said, and he said he was heading downstate if that would help and then he asked if there was a reward out, and I said, "Mister, not in this life," and he just laughed, and when he shifted through the gears I could feel the engine strain against the weight of all those beef cattle in back. In the sideview mirror I could see the pink nose of one steer through the wooden slats, and I believe it was he who bawled so loudly and so often, jailed and crowded in like that. And the driver asked me, right out of the blue, if I supported a death penalty in this state for noisy livestock and, when I stared at him like he was nuts, he said it was only a joke to help take my mind off whatever I'd done and was running from, no matter how horrible it was. He said, "Hey, I'm betting against the odds that there's an ounce of decency in everyone," which is why, he said, he was keeping a clean conscience and helping with my escape.

PAYMENT

In Payment one winter, the county budget exhausted, the roads went unplowed, packed down instead so that by late March the snowmobilers could reach up and touch the blinking yellow light that hangs in the middle of town. Think of it—three hundred inches of annual snowfall. Hey, as I said to my friend Rail, like it or not, that's what puts us on the map.

He's collecting unemployment while he writes a novel, his first. I advised him originally to set it somewhere warm and mysterious, like the Bermuda Triangle, but he refused, saying enough disappears right here. Like dogs and drunk husbands and single women, though sometimes they surprise you by returning. Sometimes.

I came back. Having said, "Adios Motherfuckers" to this town, I fully expected to stay gone, hell-bent on getting far enough south to where I didn't have to live anymore in a house trailer with a ladder leaning permanently against the side so I could climb up nights after work at Sawmillers and shovel the roof before it caved in and smothered us all. Meaning me and my ex-wife who might be dead now for all I know, though from other things, I suspect. If I hear someday that she is, I won't have to feel like it was all my fault.

I stayed away one year to the day, studying nights at a community college to become a TV meteorologist. Rail made it to only the tenth grade, which is why he uses me as a resource. I tell him what I learned there isn't worth a shit unless he's writing about the weather which, up here, is the main topic of conversation most days.

"Nah," Rail says, "I guess not," but he keeps calling with the goddamnedest questions. Like what do I think happens to kid stars like the Little Rascals—Alfalfa and Waldo and that cute little girl they were always hitting on, what's her name? Right, Darla. I tell him that they get old, same as you and me, I tell him, same as people who were never famous except, as Andy Warhol said, for maybe fifteen minutes.

"You had your fifteen yet?" Rail asks me and I tell him the truth, that I have, more than twenty years ago when I was nineteen and still had my hair and was mistaken in a restaurant for Sam of Sam the Sham and the Pharaohs. It was a waitress with heavy blue eyeliner who asked, then stood giggly and cracking her gum while I autographed her wrist with ink she swore she would never wash off. My date told me all through dinner that I was nuts, but we ate gratis and I could tell she loved the attention. And what comes on the car radio first thing while we're driving back to her place? *Uno, dos, tres,/One, two, three,/Quatro.* "Wooly Bully," and I crank it up and I can see her tapping both feet on the new floormat and I'm suddenly as happy as I've ever been in my life. When she slides close to me across the smooth green vinyl seat and punches in the cigarette lighter and reaches into my shirt pocket for a Lucky Strike, I know that I am blessed, her skirt riding high up on her thighs. Her thighs, I tell Rail, look just like silk, soft and white in the magic light of the dashboard.

Seems like material he might be able to use he says, and thanks me for the personal details and hangs up.

What I don't tell him is that I woke cramped early the next morning in her bed. It wasn't even fall yet, but during the night the temperature plunged and it had snowed like hell. I thought, while sliding barefoot into my shoes, that I could explain to her about unusual polar shifts, wondering if she had a globe somewhere in that claptrap of a house. A blue rotating globe. And I almost asked, but her eyes were closed from too much hashish and I had one screamer of a hangover anyhow, so I walked outside to the back porch to clear my head, the wind blowing cold and hard and straight into my face. It felt good. But when I turned around to go back in, all these shiny black hairs were stuck to the snow on the screen door. Hairs exactly the length and color of mine, hundreds of them, like a shedding dog had leaned there, waiting to be let in. I mean, imagine that moment, knowing that in a year or two you were going to look like shit, when less than twelve hours earlier you'd been mistaken for Sam the Sham. And nobody to commiserate with—that's the last thing on earth you tell the woman you've just made love to for the first time. Believe me, the very fucking last goddamn thing.

Before the big snows arrive you can see teenagers smooching in their cars or pickups behind the diner where, last year, I used to fill in nights maybe two or three times a month. If I shut off the light above the sink in the back room, more often than not I'd see Carl Ogden, a twenty-two-year-old sicko, trying to get some younger girl to touch his wang. Some people around here still feel sorry for him—when he was a little kid he was bitten in the eye by a bat. There's this superstition that red hair attracts them, which Carl has, a full curly head of it. A carrot-top. Obviously he did not die from rabies, which was the real scare, but the eye turned an even lighter blue and is now almost white like an albino. One look, when he was seventeen and desperate to leave Payment, and the army rejected him. He told me one Sunday, sipping coffee at the counter at 1:30 in the morning, only the two of us there, that he had a killer new line. Field-tested and successful. "Listen up," he said, and described how he kept a baby food jar in the glove compartment of his pickup. That was the key, he said, that jar. He said you drink a few quick brews and take the jar out and, in your saddest, most sincere voice, explain to the babe how desperately you need to be jerked-off for the spermbank because you've got this rare disease that's making you sterile.

"Copisce?" he said, and I just walked out from behind the counter to unlock the door for him. You don't endorse that kind of crude stupidity by even smiling. I tell you it's pitiful the way some kids are raised in Payment, kids who don't ever leave and spook you by what they say.

"Good writing should make your reader's knees go weak," I say to Rail who says back to me, "Fine, right," but he wants me to be more concrete—he wants me to outline for him what he should do in chapter three. He's stuck, he says, but he feels good nonetheless about his hero who he claims is based loosely on me, a pensive and soft-spoken local weatherman whose predictions are always right on the money. He knows, for example, right to the half-inch how much snow will fall each night. "But unlike you," Rail says, "*unlike* you, he has an eighteen-month-old daughter who requires special breathing apparatus because she's had scarlet fever and naps upstairs in an oxygen tent." He says he made that whole part up in his head. Rail's no dummy.

"Bobby," he says, "this is going to be the saddest fucking novel you've ever read."

It already is. While he talks I'm thinking about the children I never had and about the wife I did who confessed to me in the car I'd driven into a snowbank and couldn't get started, that she had never really loved me, never. And this after eleven years of marriage. Which is not an easy thing to hear, the engine turning over more and more slowly, the temperature outside at minus thirty. Nobody this far north needs to exaggerate with windchill—I'm talking straight degrees. Not the kind of night you decide finally to walk away from it all, if you know what I mean. You're afraid to even get out to light a flare, afraid you'll lose what little heat is still trapped in the car. You try the headlights again and you know, from the dim glimmer of a halo, that the battery is almost out of juice. There you are, forced to hug enough warmth from one another to stay alive. I say "you" because I cannot talk about it any other way. This, for me, is very shaky ground. It makes me crazy just to remember how much I had wanted to kiss her after we climbed into the back seat and huddled together, her stammering every couple of minutes, "Oh, God, oh, God," whom she thanked over and over for the drunk snowmobilers He sent just in time to our rescue. We glided across miles of glittering white fields on snow as high as the fencelines, then along Highway 662 to the County End Bar where I drank shots of Jack Daniels until the world blurred so completely I could have been anywhere, on fucking Mars. Which is how I stayed for almost two months, until spring and detox when I finally sobered up. My wife had disappeared and I'd lost my job at Sawmillers and Sons, the local lumberyard. I refer to her as my ex, though I guess legally we're not divorced since I never signed the papers. Mail can be awfully slow in Payment, especially if Ray Simmons, our postmaster, holds it back. He's got his own dead-letter box, a big one for a town of four hundred, full of what he knows is bad news people on the edge can do without. He'll let you sort through it if you want, but I never have. I ask you, what's the point?

Rail is originally from Vancouver. He's used to cold climates. He's only twenty-five and a carpenter by trade, and a good one. He's French. And, if I haven't mentioned it, Rail goes 6'4" and has a hook nose and a bushy blond mustache. That's not important to me, but he believes a writer needs to get down in black and white what people look like. He says the whole world is reflected in a single face. "Yeah," I tell him, "God's face," which sounds pretty glib, I know, to a young novelist who is battling every day just to cover the basics, so I listen while he gives me an earful, while he bitches me out. He says I'm crimping his style. He says I've gotten unjustly short-tempered lately and that he won't be calling for any feedback for quite a while.

The phone rings ten minutes later and I answer saying, "Look, I'm sorry," and the voice on the other end says, "Apology accepted," but it's not Rail. It's the yard foreman at Sawmillers calling to hire me back, but at a lower wage. Seems like some of the younger guys have enlisted. Not Carl Ogden, but lesser versions of him, kids who say, "Fucking-A, get me out of this place," and who have never pledged to anything in their brief lives that didn't have four-wheel drive and monster tires and, rubberbanded to their visors, pinups with monster tits. But I don't want to see them die, which is what I'm thinking about the very next day on my forklift, moving stacks of plywood from here to there. I'm wearing a yellow hardhat and driving a machine I think resembles a tank. And at the end of one of the avenues of cold, and yes, snowy sunlight, the plotless movement of a squirrel running this way and that way. Three guys with shovels raised above their heads are after it, hooting like madmen from hell. Although I know those aren't gasmasks they have on, only masks against the cold, I'm certain at that moment that war is everywhere, even in Payment, and that someday there will be a monument per se, a headstone of pink mottled marble in the park by the swings. Not with names like Aberlich or Abrams or Ackerman or Adamczak, but something farther down in the alphabet. Maybe only one name. Maybe Jimmy Tatch whose dented black lunchpail I found and opened during morning coffee break. Nothing inside but an empty, crumpled up pack of smokes. I suppose I'll remember him in uniform if he's the one sent back in a box from a war. If not, he'll always be the asshole who one day pelted his own dog so hard in the ear with a snowball that the damn dog went deaf. Whimpered and looked around at all the silence and never made another sound.

"Tough to sort things out," I tell Rail, who is red-eyed already and paying for the tequila, the two of us huddled up at the end of the empty bar with the salt shaker and lemon wedges. He says that he was game when he first started, but that the writing and the winter have combined this year to wear him down—not exactly the words he used, but it's what he meant when he said, "I look like shit, I feel like shit, I must be shit."

"Bottoms up," I say, because I've known the feeling well, so we clink shot glasses with the kind of idiot determination that signals we're already half in the bag and the night is young and we still have a million stupendous insights to deliver before Stony, the bartender, shuts us off. Which is all fine by me on a Thursday night in early March. We're safe here, me and Rail, unless somebody else arrives and pulls out some weed or worse, something that can really fuck us up.

Rail is still on his feces motif—he says, "Bobby, old hat, editors don't give two shits about me." He says his unemployment is about to run out and that his Firebird is a junkheap and that he'll honest to Christ be up Shit Creek without the proverbial paddle again by the end of this month. Jack-shit, shit out of luck, scared shitless, shitfaced, shit on a stick or on a shingle. Rail uses them all—he has a penchant for local phrases like that.

I can't argue. I say, "It's true, there's a lot of shit in this world, Rail," and he says back, "Yeah," and that you can't squeeze ten pounds of it into a five-pound bag. He's much further into the sauce than me, but still making good sense, and I know his vision isn't too seriously impaired because it's him who turns on his stool and sees Jeaneah Pezzell has just stepped in out of the cold. Jesus, I think, when Rail nudges me and I see her for the first time in twenty years. Jeaneah

Pezzell, the snow carnival queen the only year there ever was a carnival in Payment. 1970. I still have the poster of her posing in a bathing suit and high heels and a bright red beret in front of that transparent blue ice sculpture of a mermaid. I've examined the poster close-up, always figuring that some-one good must have airbrushed the negative to get out those goosebumps I saw that day all over her body when she stepped for maybe thirty seconds max out of her bathrobe. I was never so turned-on in my life. And I see them again on her arms when she takes off her scarf and full-length parka and sits down right next to me and orders hot apple cider and rum. In the grainy deep mirror behind the bar I can see she still has that same great cleavage and I am wordless to de-scribe to Rail how I feel when she crosses the room and leans right over the jukebox which is so seldom played anymore. Old rock-and-roll tunes.

She is absolutely stunning from this distance, and I am once again ashamed to be me, my mouth half open, my bald head perspiring now under the thin membrane of pale, smoky light.

"Whew," is all Rail can get out, but it has nothing to do with the perfume that floats from the empty space above her bar stool. It is an expression of awe, like he has suddenly lost his breath, and I nod in agreement, as though I've been chasing the ghost of her my entire life. Which is what too many winters in Payment can do to a guy—make him fall in love with phantoms. But for once it's a woman in the flesh come home after all this time. Who knows what for. And wearing a sleeveless dress. You'd think the dogwoods were in bloom. But you can see through the plate-glass window that the faded pink is only neon reflected on the snow.

Still, I can almost feel spring in my bones, and I predict to Rail that it's K-4, "Wooly Bully," that's about to play. But she punches nothing in. She has turned her back on the jukebox, and she's not snapping her fingers or mouthing lyrics—she has zoomed in on me now after an exaggerated double take, and she says, from not ten feet away, "Bobby Shefferly?"

"That's right," I say, "it's me, the very same," and after
Jeaneah and I are done with the big hugs, I introduce Rail as
the only writer-at-large in Payment. The only writer ever.
She laughs—we all do—and we gather our drinks and pow-
wow around a table and shoot the breeze until Rail fades and
decides to leave so he can get some sleep and get back to his
novel first thing when he wakes. We can feel the frigid air all
the way down here as he opens the door and stands there a
few seconds and waves.

Not another person has come in, incredible as that seems,
though we all heard Phil Clark's sleddogs barking as they
passed about an hour ago. And Stony is slouched in a chair in
the back, watching TV, the reception perfect from his satellite dish. I don't call him—I walk right behind the bar and
pour another couple drinks. We've slowed way down, trying
to pace ourselves, and I can see clearly a dusting of new snow
on the windshield of Jeaneah's car, a late model Chevrolet. I
know she's going to follow me home and spend the night. And
she knows it. And Stony has come out to tell me that a guy on
David Letterman has just stopped the spinning blades of an
electric fan with his tongue. "Stupid Human Tricks," he says.
Then he says, "Stupid is right, for a few short minutes of
fame."

"Fifteen minutes," I want to say, "fifteen for each of us in a
lifetime." But Stony is shaking his head and already walking
away. Jeaneah has not heard us. She has draped her scarf
around her shoulders, and she has taken a compact out of her
pocketbook and is staring into its small round mirror, circling her mouth. I notice, when I sit back down, that the
lipstick she has just put on is deep red. Which changes her,
and when she lets down her hair she is truly a stranger, as I
am to her when I reach slowly over and cover her hand with
mine. I know Rail could never describe the complexity of this
scene—two nobodies alone in a bar before closing, staring
into each other's eyes. Maybe he'd get that part. What he'd
miss, because he is still young and was not born here, is why
we're so silent suddenly, afraid to even speak. Whoever does

will say something sad about who we were once, and the other will nod. And not to be misled, we'll agree that this isn't love, but rather a place where we met up again near the end of a certain winter in Payment and talked some about her reasons for leaving, about mine for having stayed on.

PART 3

From Here to There

Nelson Pelky said to my father, "Personally, I don't give a rat's ass. If it were up to me, I'd deliver the mail." But it wasn't, so he passed our house and waved to my father, who was watching out the kitchen window and did not wave back.

The town was growing and Louis Darby was replaced by a new postmaster from downstate who announced that his carriers would abide by U.S. Postal regulations or be fired, rural route delivery included. At first my father said, "Screw that noise." He'd lived at this same address for over twenty years, and Nelson Pelky knew him well, and he knew me, too, and my mother, who had recently left us, but he said it meant his job, and if he couldn't see the numbers marked clearly on the box or on the house or on the garage, then he couldn't leave the mail. "I know, I know, goddamnit," Nelson had said when my father argued common sense. "I know all that, Tommy, and I'm on your side, but I can't stop here."

I was eating lunch, and my father saw me peeking at him and he stood suddenly, and with his back to me he said, "Finish up and come on outside and help me," and he put his coffee mug on the table and lit a cigarette and nodded to me to make sure I'd heard him, and I said, "Yes." I said, "I'm all done," and I wiped my mouth and got up and put my dish and glass in the sink and followed him down the back stairs and out into the garage. That's where he stored the paint, the gallon cans dusty and dented, and you could tell the different colors by what had dripped across the labels.

"Here," he said, and handed me a can of bright red. Then he picked up a brush that was very stiff, and he bent the bristles back and forth until they softened some, and then he turned the brush handle down and slid it into his back pocket.

"Stirrer," he said, and he reached for one higher up, but it was stuck to the wooden shelf. I started to shake the can of paint but he said, "No, don't do that," as though the cover might fly off. But it wouldn't have. It took him going almost all the way around the lid with a screwdriver, and when the lid did come off, there was this skin he had to puncture, a rubbery red skin, but the paint underneath was fine, and I liked the smell.

Mostly my father didn't give two hoots about the mail, but he was waiting now for a letter from my mother, so he gave in and painted those numbers, 335, across the two white doors. It took him a good half hour, and when he stood back I joked, "A blind man could see those from the road."

"From Lansing," he said, but I didn't get what he meant, and I said, "That's a long way," and all he said back was, "Yeah, a long way," and he walked off after turning and heaving the empty can across the dirt road and into the ditch. I moved up closer to the numbers, and they were much taller than me, and I was tall for twelve years old.

"Yeah," I yelled, "for sure they'll see these in Lansing," but my father let it drop, saying nothing. Then I heard him say, "Bastards," as he dabbed the metal flag on the mailbox with what little paint he had left on his brush. He left the flag up so it would dry by the time Nelson Pelky stopped the next morning, which he did, but only to ease the flag down. I could tell it was still sticky by the way he rubbed his thumb and fingers together. He waved to me, sitting on the porch stairs, and I yelled, "Hi Mr. Pelky," and after he drove off my father stepped outside and touched my head, and I looked up at him and said, "No mail."

"You sure?" he said, and I said, "Maybe tomorrow," but I knew what he was waiting for wouldn't arrive, not this time, most likely not ever. My mother didn't want him finding her, which is why she left so late at night the way she did, my father working the graveyard shift at the sheet metal plant. She sat on the edge of my bed for a long time, explaining nothing but saying over and over how she loved me very much, and that someday I'd understand. Then she kissed me and rubbed my back real gently and I didn't cry, not right then I didn't. And she said for me not to let anyone in except my father, and she locked the door behind her when a car drove into the driveway, killing its lights. "I'll be back for you," she shouted from outside. "I promise I'll be back." And then I heard her say, "Oh, God," and then the trunk slam, and then the two car doors, and she was gone.

That happened over three weeks ago, and I missed her something terrible, but I was awful mad at her, too. My father had lots of sick days coming, and he started taking them, and his vacation time, too, so he had over a month to stay home, and he spent most of it near the phone, which almost never rang. Once a wrong number, and once my Grandpa Eby called, and all my father said was, "Lynette's not here. No." He said "no" again, and a third time, and then he hung up. When it rang a few seconds later, he didn't answer it.

And Nelson Pelky left only bills, which went unpaid. And my father started drinking more, and he didn't shave often or go to the laundromat. All the towels were dirty, and it got so

I'd have to dry off with a T-shirt after getting out of the shower. When his good friend Paul Tremblay stopped by late one night he told my father, "You look like shit."

"Get out," my father said. "Get the hell out, unless you know where she is."

"I don't," Paul said, "nobody in town does," and he said he didn't know who the guy was either. Then he said, "Listen to me, Tommy, I'm no goddamn private eye," and my father grabbed him by the shirt front and backed him hard against the refrigerator, my father's elbow wedged under Paul's chin, all this right in front of me, and I shouted, "Stop, stop it," and this time I *was* crying, bawling my eyes out, and I sat down on the floor in the corner of the kitchen, my face in my hands, and when I looked up a few minutes later my father was crying, too, and Paul was gone. My father tried to talk, but he could not. Then finally he said, "She'll write to us, and we'll go pick her up, wherever she is. She'll come home."

But I knew if she did, it wouldn't be to stay. She'd left before, I don't know how many times, but always for only one day and always to the Cottage Motel. My father even learned to joke about it, saying, "Your mother's at the Cottage," like it was a vacation spot or something, like she'd gone off to the lake or the mountains for a rest. But the motel was just down Route 28, right outside of town, and it was cheap and real dingy. Paul Tremblay once told me, "A woman who issues a man his walking papers don't just go to the Cottage. She ups and leaves town." Which my mother never did. Until now. Now it was all different. Now there was another man involved.

If my father found him, he'd beat him up bad, maybe kill him. The guy most likely didn't know my father could dead-lift over 500 pounds. He proved it one year at the state fair, coming right out of the crowd, and he won fifty bucks. People clapped, and when he stepped down from the platform he was counting his money. Then he put it in his wallet and smiled and rubbed his fingers through my hair. My mother was holding his shirt, which he put on and buttoned, and she held his arm when we walked off across the fairgrounds because that's when we were all happy.

Maybe I was five then, small enough to still ride on his shoulders. I ate cotton candy and hardly made a peep up there, watching all the different colored lights on the amusement rides and the people passing and smiling up at me. My mother would nod to them and reach up and pat my bare leg. She'd say, "Having fun?" and I'd say, "Yes," but that was before they hurt each other.

My father was first. He hit her one evening right before supper, I don't even know what for, and then he stared for a long time at his hand, stared like it wasn't a part of him, and when my mother finally turned from the cupboard, her nose was bleeding from one nostril. She wiped the blood away with the back of her hand. "It's okay," she said to me, and she sounded very calm. "Your father didn't mean it."

"No," he said, "I didn't, I didn't mean it," and if he meant to say something else, it did not come. She spoke first. She said to him, "Turn down the burners," and he did, all the way to off, and all with his left hand, the one that hadn't struck her, and she left to go lie down on the couch in the living room, pulling the white afghan over her, snug to her chin. "I love your mother," he said. He said, "I'm sorry," loud enough for her to hear, but he did not go to her. He walked outside, and I stayed seated at the table. I turned my head and I could see my mother, and she was shaking real bad. "Mom?" I said, and she got quiet, so I called her again, and she said, "He didn't mean it, Sweetheart," which I knew was true, and that he really was sorry, but that nothing in the world could ever change what had happened.

My mother slept finally, and I cleared the unused dishes from the table, then the silverware, knowing we wouldn't sit together as a family, not that night we wouldn't. I drank a glass of cold water and ate peach halves right from the can and, without saying goodnight to anyone, I went to bed. My window was open halfway, and I could hear my father singing "Jamaica Farewell," his favorite Harry Belafonte song. I

wondered if my mom was listening. She loved it when my
father sang, and so did I. He had a beautiful, sad voice, and I
hummed along to the words, my cheek kind of vibrating on
the pillow:

> I'm sad to say I'm on my way,
> I won't be back for many a day,
> My heart is down, my head is turning around,
> I have to leave a little girl in Kingston Town.

Now she was gone to Texas. That was the postmark on the
certified letter the lawyer sent. It came the day my father
returned to work, this time on the day shift, so I wouldn't
have to be alone at night. Nelson Pelky let me sign for the
letter—he said he owed my father that much, but he seemed
nervous, so I said to him, "I'll be sure he gets it." Mr. Pelky
nodded and drove off. I knew he could get into trouble if I
opened it, but I did anyway. My mother was filing for divorce
and asking for custody—my full name was right there in
black and white among all those legal terms. I slid the letter
back in the envelope and folded it into my back pocket. Then
I walked around back of the house and lined up a bunch of
empty beer bottles at the edge of the lawn and got the .22 out
of my father's closet and racked the first round into the chamber. Then I filled the clip and, outside, I steadied the rifle on
the porch railing and sighted down that long barrel and
popped one bottle after the other without a miss. A crow flew
overhead, and I took aim on it, too, but it was way out of
range, gliding downwind with the heavy clouds.

It was feeling a lot like fall, and I spun around and, from
the hip, I fired into the metal drum my father used sometimes
for burning papers and boxes. And I went around front to the
road, and although I did not squeeze the trigger, I pretended
to pepper the mailbox with a million holes, blow it right off
its post, and then shoot it some more on the ground like it
was a wounded and dangerous animal. But all I did was walk
up slowly and lower the shiny red flag with the barrel tip, as
though there had been no mail. "It sure ain't the goddamn

numbers we painted," my father would most likely say when
he got home, and I'd say back, "Nope, they can read those
from the state capital," and he'd smile and nod to me and say,
"Yep," and I'd wish, more than anything in the world, that
my mother had written a letter of forgiveness, saying that she
was sorry, too, and that she'd come home now to talk it all
through.

My father did not want to grow even one day older without
her, but he knew what was what. In his heart he did. Twice
this last week he'd said to me, "You're all I've got now," but I
knew if they got him into court, he'd lose me, too. If the judge
asked me who I'd rather live with I'd say, "Both of them." I'd
tell the truth and say I didn't like my mother running away
all the time and that my father sometimes scared me with his
temper, but that he cooked all my meals and played catch
with me in the backyard and, at night, over an open fire, we'd
roast marshmallows, and he'd tell some funny jokes and
stories and name the constellations. And if they asked, I'd say
my mother had some nerve saying my father wasn't fit to
raise me.

He'd promised to take me to see *Ben Hur* when it came to
Munising, about a half-hour away, and when he got home
from work one day he said, "Let's go." He said, "Step on it,
Buster Brown, we're on our way to the movies."

On the drive over he talked to me a little about my mother.
He said life was too short to fritter away, waiting for a
woman, even your own wife, if she couldn't make up her
mind. It's not like he'd adjusted to being without my mom,
but he did seem to be doing better. Until halfway through the
show he did, right after Ben Hur won the chariot race. I could
tell that my father loved that scene and, I guess not thinking
about where he was, he lit a cigarette. Nobody was close to us
in the front row, and nobody shouted down for him to put the
cigarette out. And he didn't, not even when the usher told
him to. Instead, my father took a long, slow drag and tilted
his head back and exhaled, the smoke blue and floating

through the beam of the projector light. I said to him, "It's okay to smoke in the lobby," but he got mad and flicked the butt up at the big screen, and it was as though he'd spooked those six white horses who reared and whinnied, Ben Hur straining against them, heavy on the reins.

"Let's go," I said, "come on, Dad," and when I turned my head I could see the manager coming, his flashlight on. He shouldn't have shined it in our eyes because when he did my father grabbed it and stood up and threw *it* at the screen, too, and the light made a loud clunk when it bounced off and hit the floor. He said to the manager, "In Rome they'd hang scum like you up by the balls, they'd feed you to the swine."

Right then the theater lights along both walls came on, and the projector stopped, and the manager said, "Please, just leave." The usher was bigger than me, but I was ready to fight him if I had to, the two of us duking it out in the aisle. But he made no move when my father shoved the manager, first with one hand and then much harder with both hands, knocking him on his can on the worn, red carpet. My father reached for the ticket stubs in his shirt pocket and threw them in the manager's face and crouched down and whispered something I couldn't hear, and then we left quickly through the EXIT door. I thought sure the cops would be waiting, but they were not. It was still partly light out, but the moon was up already and almost full, and my father was a few steps ahead of me.

"Drop that box of popcorn," he said, "and come on," and he started to run, and by the time we got to the car he was out of breath, but he said, "Get on the floor in back and stay down." Which I did until we hit Route 28 and he said, "It's all clear," and I climbed into the front seat.

It was dark now and the dash lights glowed green. My father pushed in the lighter and reached for his pack of Chesterfields between us on the seat.

"I wish I could undo a lot that I've done in my life," he said, "but I've drifted too far downstream to paddle back now."

The lighter popped out and he lit his cigarette, and I stared straight ahead and imagined the car was a boat and that there were fish below us in the dark water where we'd lower our lines or nets. Maybe there was a lantern on the stern and behind us a village and the women waving, the way my mother used to do from the porch each morning when my father drove off to work. He'd reappear, what seemed like days later, his headlights on, and she'd have a late supper ready for him, sometimes fresh walleye or perch or a batch of bluegill fillets that Paul Tremblay would drop off on his way home from the lake. Paul Tremblay always caught fish, and he said he'd take me when I got older, but of course he never did, not once. We had never owned a boat, but here we were, drifting at night, and my father said, "It's easy, really," and I asked, "What is?" and he said, "This, just this," and he motioned to the fields flooded with moonlight and to the moon itself and the stars which were very bright and then to the two of us, and he yawned because the days had already grown shorter, and all he was doing was pointing out the obvious landscape of our lives, how we traveled from here to there, growing older, even during those few seconds it took us to cross Black Creek, which meant we were only a few minutes from home. And only one week until school started again, and maybe two months until the heavy snow, and I knew if my mother hadn't come by then, I wouldn't see her until spring. Or never, depending on what the court decided.

"We made it," my father said, same as he always did, turning into the driveway, and he hit the high beams and those red numbers seemed to waver back and forth like a buoy. He stopped and I got out to open the garage doors, and my knees were a little shaky, as though I'd stepped ashore after being out all day on a rough lake. My father did not seem to notice. He walked right past me and up the stairs and yelled for me to close the garage doors. I did, and I leaned my back against them, and I stayed like that, repeating the posture I'd seen my father take that first night he realized for certain that my mother was gone for good. And then those numbers, as though we'd had no real address all these years, no way for her to contact us if she changed her mind about Texas and whoever it was she was with there.

I wished Nelson Pelky had sent the lawyer's letter back— "Insufficient Address" or "Undeliverable" or "Deceased," whatever lie was necessary to keep the mail away, so that I wouldn't have to hide it and get blamed when my father found out, which he would, and he'd ask, "Why, why?" and I'd just shake my head like I didn't know what was wrong or right anymore, only that this was home, and I didn't want anyone, not even my mother, ruining that from somewhere else. Let her come here, I thought, and say what it was she wanted. I was exhausted from imagining what that was, and I closed my eyes and listened to the three Harry Belafonte albums my father stacked on the hi fi. He must have thought I'd gone to bed because he never called to me and when I went in after midnight, I could hear him snoring on the couch. I peeked in and he was asleep on his stomach, one hand almost touching the floor. I could see the orange of the alarm clock dial and the phone pulled up close. I knew, by morning, only the alarm would ring. He'd hit the snooze, and then again, and then he'd have to rush so's not to be late for work. As soon as he left, I'd take the receiver off the hook in case my mother called me.

And before Nelson Pelky arrived I'd grab the .22 and hide in the cellar hole across the road. Not in ambush, exactly, but if he spotted me and started toward me with another certified letter, I'd say, "You stop right there, Mr. Pelky," and I'd click off the safety so he knew I meant business, so he knew I was nobody to mess with. He'd probably call me my father's boy. Grownups did, especially teachers, whenever I'd fist fight at school. "That's a fact," I'd say, "I am," and I'd tell my father, and he'd say, "Let 'em make something of it. Let 'em say it to me."

But the only one who ever did was my mother. She'd say, "I suppose you want him to raise a hand to me, too?" which I'd never do, and my father had only done it the one time, which, like I said, had ruined everything. After that my mother seemed to dare him to do it again. She'd lift her chin and step close and say mean stuff, but he'd just slide his hands into his pockets and stand there and take it. He said to me once, "I won't forever, I won't," but I knew he would. It was him who loved her, not the other way around. When I got older and got married my wife would have to love me back. That's what I hated about my mother. Not that she ran off to Texas, but that she made it seem like my father's fault. He was no angel, that's for sure, but he could be awful kind. I'd say that to the judge, too, if they really did subpoena my father, and I'd say how he left me fresh cut slices of pumpernickel on the breadboard each morning so I could have toast with my cereal. But I figured that wouldn't matter to the law. They'd talk on and on about how I had no friends and how I was always real quiet and shy and showed no emotion, like it was some crime to be alone and keep your thoughts to yourself. But like my father said about me to the counselor at school one day, "He don't look punched or bored, now does he?" And I never was bored, and I was never hit at home. I read a lot and stayed to myself, fishing and hunting and building forts. My father would say to the court, "Is there something wrong with that?" He'd say, "Goddamn it, answer me," but nobody would, and I knew that's what they'd all want to see, my father's sudden temper, so they'd have grounds to snatch me as far away from him as they could. That's what Paul Tremblay told me one night when we were outside by ourselves. He said, "If you're the man, then poof, in your face. In this state the woman reigns."

So it was probably best the hearing went on without my father. He knew nothing about it and dropped me off at school on his way to work, same as always. He small-talked about the weather and how we needed to put up another five cords of wood for the stove, and about how there was a good fight on TV that night—lightweights. "About your size," he said, and flicked out a soft jab to my shoulder, and then another before he covered up, both arms hugging the steering wheel, forehead wedged between his fists. "Never make an

easy target," he said. "Give them as little as possible to hit."
But I knew he'd left himself wide open this time, and that
I was to blame. My mother and her lawyer would throw
shot after shot, give him a real pounding. And the decision?
Custody of me to my mother, just like Paul Tremblay had
predicted.

All day in the back row I wondered if she'd be there when I
got home, waiting with the verdict. There was no car in the
driveway, but I stood in the road awhile, watching the dust
kicked up by the schoolbus tires, and I could see Kevin St.
Germain and Carl Thunstrom flipping me the bird out the
back window. Usually I'd yell something at those dopes, but
not today. Today I nodded, like you win, you're right.

My mother was seated at the kitchen table, her hands
folded on top, folded like she'd been praying or listening to
someone talk at her for a long time. Her hair had grown past
her shoulders and she was wearing a new dress, and lipstick,
and from where I was standing I could see her feet under the
table, her high heels.

"It's just like your father not to show up, to tell his side,"
she said. "It's just like him." Then she opened her pocketbook
and pulled out a folded paper and asked, "Do you know what
this is?"

"Yes," I said, "it says you can take me away."

"It's all wrong," she said, "the whole thing, me sitting here.
There's a limit," she said, "and after that it's all wrong, everything's wrong, wrong. But I'm never coming back here to live,
and after the divorce is final, I'll marry again, right away."

And then she told me about Texas and about a man named
Will Roop who she loved enough to be happy and who would
adopt me and give me his name. She said I could meet him
when he came to pick her up, but I said no. And I asked if he'd
been in this house, and she said, yes, in the kitchen, right here
where your father hit me that time. And I wanted to hit her,
too, just walk over and slap her good and tell her, get out, get
out of here. But I just stood there and she said, "Those numbers on the garage, is that where we lived?"

"Yes," I said, "335. It's how you have to address everything now, or it doesn't arrive."

"All those years," she said, "and I never even knew where I lived. On a county road in northern Michigan."

"I want to stay here," I said, and I paused, and I don't know why, but I said to her, "They can see those numbers all the way to Lansing."

"Yes," she said, "you're officially listed; you exist on the map." Then she said, "Put down your books," and I did. And she said, "Now come sit next to me," and I crossed the kitchen and sat down and thought, when I looked at her close up, that if my father were to appear right now, my mother would stay forever. She would. But it was Will Roop who stood in the doorway, older than my father and not a big man, and wearing cowboy boots. I hadn't heard the car pull in, but I could hear it idling now.

"Will Roop," my mother said, "this is my son, and he does not want to come with us."

"Correction," Will Roop said. "There's nothing in those papers about 'want to.' He can want to or not when he's eighteen. Or he can want to, but don't you listen. Don't give in, or you'll never see him again."

I gave Will Roop a hate stare, and he looked down at the floor, and my mother said to him, "I'll be right out," and he didn't argue. He turned and shut the door quietly, then the screen door behind him.

"Here's my phone number," she said, and wrote it on a napkin. "You call me. You call when you decide to come live with us." I thought, by the way her lips opened and stayed that way a minute, that she was going to describe Texas, but she didn't.

"Okay," I said, "I will," and she didn't start crying when she hugged me, and without saying anything else she got up and left, quick as that.

From the kitchen window I watched the car back onto the road, then drive down the wrong side to the mailbox. Will Roop reached into it and raised the metal flag and drove away. I knew my father would be home soon, but I waited a good fifteen minutes before going out there.

My father's name was on the envelope, and under it, in red lipstick, 335, and nothing else. I opened it and read the letter which asked my father not to contest the divorce, and if he needed to contact her it had to be through the courts. Never by phone, never face to face. She said she loved Will Roop, though she didn't mention his name, and I knew that was a lie, which seemed okay in a way. And she said that she had never really loved my father, which I hoped wasn't true. She was still angry, writing that letter right here on our kitchen table, probably. I figured the end of something like this needed an honest distance, a real stamp and postmark and return address, the kind of letter Nelson Pelky could deliver without risking a thing. I could smell the perfume in the lipstick when I crumpled the letter up and stuck it in my pocket. And I could see when my father's car was in sight that he had Paul Tremblay with him, as he often did on Friday nights.

"You been with a lady," Paul said, putting his arm around my shoulder. "Hey, Tommy," he said, "your kid's got himself a dame."

"Probably Janet Knoble," I said, "sometimes she stinks up the whole bus."

"Women do that when they're away from home," Paul joked. "They leave their scent for you to remember them by, ain't that right, Tommy?" My father didn't answer, and Paul laughed again and reached for the football on the lawn and said, "Slant pattern," and I cut just a few yards in front of him, and when I caught the wobbly pass he yelled, "Yes, yes, yes," while my father walked away, not to check the mail, but to kind of stare off down the road.

"He'll get over it," Paul said, when I came back to hand him the ball, "and you will, too," and I nodded to show I understood. We both watched my father for a few seconds more before Paul barked out another play, and this time I ran the deep route, as fast and far from the two of them as I could.

WISH PENNIES

Whatever we thought after my father died didn't matter. My mother said there were strict rules about what to do with the ashes of suicides, but she didn't tell us what those rules were, and we didn't ask. We stayed out of her bedroom, even though that's where the TV was and, on her bureau beside it, the box with the ashes.

My adopted brother Howard didn't like my mother. She'd started drinking again and Howard said she was talking crazy, which I guess she was and had been, ever since my father killed himself that winter in the garage. But I didn't want to discuss it anymore—I wanted to give her some time to figure things out.

I never asked to see the note my father left in the car, which, sometime during the early morning hours, finally ran out of gas. I remember, a few weeks later, that it was Howard who started it and backed it slowly out into the driveway after dark, his foot, every couple seconds, tapping the brakes. And I remember how he moved that single match flame back and forth along the dashboard, illuminating the plastic Saint Christopher. He said he was testing for fumes. My mother whispered to me that no, he wasn't. She said he was purifying the car of its evil spirits.

Later I told Howard what she had said, and he said back to me, "She's halfway around the bend already, no kidding, Wayne, she is, that's no lie," and that same day he told her that we should sprinkle the ashes over the ground of my father's nursery, but she said to him, quoting John Donne, *For God's sake hold your tongue, and let me love.* Unlike my father, she had been four years to college out east and had her degree and read books like that all the time.

"She doesn't know how to love," Howard said to me, "she never did," which really meant that she hadn't loved him as much after I was born. That's how my father had explained it to me, and it became more and more obvious after he died. That was in 1959, the year Howard got his driver's license. He was seventeen but he'd been driving the tractor and pickup around the property for years. He was three years older than me and he liked to get away from the house now, away from my mother. After school let out in June, he started asking to use the car more. If she'd say no, he'd ask me to ask her and she'd nod okay and then she'd say, "You two be careful," but of course Howard never would. He'd be furious and drive way too fast, gripping the steering wheel with one hand and fiddling with the radio and saying how someday he'd track down his real mother and ask her her last name and change his to that. I asked him if we'd still be brothers and he got quiet for a while and then he said, "Sure, sure we will," that that was forever.

Howard had always worked with my father summers in the nursery, so this summer he didn't have a job. My mother sold off all the stock to a landscape architect from Grand Rapids—shrubs and flowering crabs and forsythia and honeysuckle, you name it, and after a full week, when that crew had finished digging and loading, we had a field out back of the house with nothing growing. Even the birds disappeared. One night, right after that, Howard couldn't sleep, and he came into my bedroom and shook my shoulder and whispered, "C'mon, hurry up," and I got dressed and found him a few minutes later standing on the back porch, staring out to where the nursery had been. It wasn't quite first light and we were barefoot and I was shivering a little, but I followed him, and when we finally stopped, maybe a hundred yards from the house, I said to him, "I'm glad we didn't spread his ashes out here, Mom was right."

"If we had," he said, lighting a cigarette, "those landscaping goons would have had to fight through us to get a single shovel in this ground."

"That's for sure," I said, but all I could think about, with the sun coming up, was how all those holes they'd left behind looked like so many unfinished graves.

I liked tooling around with Howard, I liked it a lot. And I was the one who suggested we stop at Thirlby's and have our own set of keys made. So we did, and after that we rarely even asked my mother—we simply took the car, sometimes to go to the movies or to the A&W out on Route 39 or over to the shore of Lake Michigan where we'd park and listen to the waves crash against the boulders. One time we drove to the demolition derby at the old fairgrounds in Manton, and, before it started, Howard had pointed at a black Packard like ours, a two-door, and he said, "That one," and sure enough, it was the last car running, though only in reverse. But mostly he didn't point out anything, he just drove that whole summer. And the only time he'd scare me was when he'd pull into the lot of the Crossroads Bar, always at night, and he'd park way away from the other cars, leaving the engine idling while he went inside for a six-pack of Stroh's to go. And every single time I'd imagine my father closing the garage doors behind him and rolling down the car windows and staring through this same windshield at the wall where he always hung his pruning saws and shears and, on that single wooden dowel, his faded red hat with the long visor. I'd wonder if that's where he wrote his suicide note, and if, before killing the headlights, he knew it was March 10th, the only square on the calendar not penciled in with names and figures and telephone numbers. Howard had told me that settling on death was plenty to fill up any day. He said there probably wasn't much reason to schedule anything else. He wasn't being smart when he said that. He loved my father because he played no favorites.

Coming back to the car, the six-pack under his arm, he'd always say the same thing, like it was the first time he'd gotten served. He'd say, "Got it," and he'd put the beer between us on the seat and throw his Levi jacket over it and tell me to keep down. Then he'd drive slowly onto county road 31, shift into second, and say, "Okay," and I'd get up and he'd really punch it. He called my father's car the perfect getaway car, lots of horses under the hood and, as he said, when it idled, it never stalled out. "Ask Dad," I almost said one time, but it's like Howard knew what I was thinking and he cranked up the radio and sang along to Del Shannon's "Runaway" while the glow-green needle of the speedometer climbed past eighty, then eighty-five, and he yelled over to me, "This is living, little brother," but he backed off when the car started to shimmy and I could see him fighting the steering wheel and someone's high beams approaching fast and, for that half second it took for the two cars to pass, he was staring at me and I could see that he was crying.

My mother said we were putting the rec room on hold—no Ping-Pong table or bumper pool. She said, after paying in all these years, my father's life insurance policy was worthless. "So pointless," she said, "so pointless and homely and foolhardy." I asked her if we were poor now and she said no, not yet, but that she'd already considered returning to teach nights at the community college. Howard said they'd never take her, no way, that she was nuts and a drunk, but I got mad at him and said no she wasn't.

We'd been sitting on the railroad trestle, about thirty feet above the river, our legs dangling, and Howard was on his third beer. Each time he finished one, he'd hold the bottle's long neck between his thumb and index finger and carefully drop it and catch it between his feet and then he'd let it go again and we'd both listen a few long seconds for the faint splash. We could never see it hit, not even with the full moon.

"She talks to herself," Howard said and I told him so did I, just not out loud, but that inside I was yakking all the time and that most likely he did too. "And anyway," I argued, "mostly she's reading poems, she's memorizing poems."

"Not poems," he said. "One poem, it's always the exact same one," which was true, and she had asked me a half-dozen times if I knew it and every time I had said no, I didn't. Then she'd come into my bedroom and sit on the edge of my bed and read me the part about *Death, be not proud*, and, before falling asleep, I'd think about how few sympathy cards had arrived in the mail, how few phone calls. I guess people were spooked about the suicide, not knowing how to respond. The only one who sent flowers to the house was Vernon Cappy, an older man who'd been in the war with my father and who never talked, a man with long gray hair combed behind his ears. He used to dig trees with my father, sometimes late at night in the headlights of the pickup, the two men working side by side, trying to get an order out. Crazy men, my mother would say, watching their silhouettes from the kitchen window. Crazy, crazy men.

I liked the way the moonlight funneled downriver to the first bend and shimmered there in the current, and I liked pressing my forehead against the cool steel railing of the trestle, taking a couple swigs off each of Howard's beers. He didn't want me drinking a whole one, not up there he didn't.

"This is the perfect place to spread his ashes," he said, "on a night like this. Know what I mean?"

"It's quiet," I said, "it's high up," and I tried to imagine how the ashes would feel on my fingers and how I would cross myself and whisper an "Our Father" as they floated down.

"Ashes to ashes," Howard said and then he paused, then continued. "Dad loved us both, Wayne, just the same, and I say it's wrong to keep his ashes in a box inside. He spent his whole life outdoors. He loved being outdoors. He's the one showed us this place, Wayne, remember?" He leaned forward a little and looked over at me and said, "Goddamn right you do."

I did remember, and clearly, though I was very young, maybe four or five years old, when he brought us. He carried a Coleman lantern, the mantle glowing bright white and hissing in the globe. It was summer then too, and he held my hand and Howard walked right behind us, holding onto my father's jacket. Really it was pretty safe up there if you were careful. As my father had said, "You'd have to jump to fall, you'd have to concentrate on it," and that's when he gave us each a penny and told us to make a wish. He said he could see in our eyes that we were good wishers but that we couldn't ever say what it was we wanted. "Wish and believe," he said, and then we threw our pennies over the railing and we listened and listened but there wasn't a sound. My father said wish pennies fell slower than God, which I figured later meant you had to wait a long time sometimes for your wish to come true. My father hadn't thrown a penny and Howard asked him why not and my father, staring out over the river, said, "Man alive, look how pretty it is out there," like this *was* his wish, to be alone with his two boys between the river and the stars. We didn't stay long though, and I remember, right before we left, how he stooped on one knee and hugged us both real tight, one in each arm, and then he pushed us a little bit away so we could see his eyes. "Always remember," he said, "always, always, always, that you can come here when you have big things to decide. They won't seem so big," he said, "and you'll feel like great thinkers." Then he got up and tousled our hair and we had to walk fast to keep up with him, to keep just inside the circle of light thrown by the lantern.

My father had been wrong. Ten years later, up on the trestle, all I felt was confused, about what he'd meant that night
and about my mother's forgetfulness, and about Howard,
mostly about him and what he'd said on the drive over about
being orphaned twice, now that my father was dead.

"Wayne," he said. "Wayne, listen to me," and he reached
over and handed me a penny, which seemed all wrong and I
said so. I said no, that I didn't believe anymore in wishes,
which was true, I didn't, though I hadn't known it until that
moment, remembering right then how hard I had squeezed
that penny the last time, wishing and wishing that my father
would never die, and believing it. I had sat next to him on the
drive home, my right hand cupped, and before we got out, I
lifted it toward Howard's nose and I said, "Smell," and he did
and he said to me, "Copper, from the penny," and I said back,
"Yeah, I know."

"Slow down," I said. Howard had his last beer between his
legs, and he kept straddling the broken white lines, drifting
into the opposite lane. I had promised him I'd steal the box of
ashes. And for the past hour we'd been driving around, not
talking, just killing time until my mother went to bed, which
we knew she had, the second time we cruised by the house,
when we saw the porch light on. We pulled into the driveway
and Howard dimmed the headlights and stopped a few feet
from the garage doors. Then he turned the engine off.

"Tomorrow," he said, "promise me you'll do it tomorrow."

"Yes," I said, "I promise," and the two of us sat there in the
dark car, the motor cooling down and ticking, not like seconds or minutes or hours, not the kind of ticking where you
waited for things to happen or not happen. No, it wasn't that,
nor the impulse to check your watch or your car clock or the
shift of the sun or the moon in the sky, but rather of something stopped, a kind of consent to the day ending, and to the
next, and the next. I knew my father did not feel that at the
end, though I still don't know why. And sitting there with
Howard, I imagined my father, who some people say I resem-

ble in looks, adding up, in his final few minutes, all the years so he could see, finally, where he'd messed up on the long-term plans of his life. I knew my mother was part of it, but that didn't matter right then. Howard hated her and my father had died and I did not want to take sides against her. I wanted to put all this behind us and go on, which I believed was possible but probably wouldn't ever happen. I knew my mother would continue to drink, and I knew deep down she'd blame Howard even after I told her it was me who took the ashes, and that Howard would not go to college in Ann Arbor as planned because my mother would need that money to live. And I knew he'd leave at the end of the summer, maybe to a college town where he'd make some friends. I figured, eventually, my mother would put a "For Sale" sign on the windshield of the Packard, and face it toward the road, and sell it, thanking the person who stopped by with the first low offer. I hoped, whenever this happened, she wouldn't mention the suicide, cheapen it any more. Yes, I thought again, things stopping, and when I couldn't hear the ticking anymore, I reached over and nudged Howard and asked him for the keys.

"Nothing doing," he said, "Uh-uh," but he was groggy and I told him I didn't want him out alone driving half drunk, or getting cold out here and turning on the heater and falling asleep. He didn't argue. He said okay, that he was coming inside too, and after we were already in the house, he went back to lock the door and to turn out the porch light. It was right under his bedroom window and he said it would keep him awake. But it wouldn't have. He was almost out on his feet, his eyes already slits. He just needed a reason not to say what he really meant, which was that he was the man of the household now, the oldest son, and he wanted to be sure, in the morning, that all of us would wake up feeling safe.

Two days later me and Howard waited for my mother in the living room while she got dressed. When she walked out she was completely in black, wearing the same suit she'd worn for the funeral, if that's what a cremation is. I had told her back then that it wasn't Catholic and she had grabbed my arm real hard and told me neither was suicide, that my father's soul was damned in that church and that anyway she had seen enough mulch and sod and black dirt in her lifetime and that my father was not going into the ground. My mother wasn't Catholic, she wasn't any faith that day when she got up from a stiff-backed chair and walked over and lifted her veil and kissed the casket, her fingertips pressing and pressing the shiny mahogany.

"Show me," she said, "you boys show me where you dropped the ashes." I was dressed in a coat and tie and Howard was too, and he opened the car door for my mother and pulled the seat forward and held her elbow as she got into the back. I sat up front with him, and when he pulled onto the road, my mother said, "Turn on your headlights and drive slowly. You lead the other cars." But there were no others. It was very early on a Friday morning, and cool, and no sun yet, and down the straightaway on county road 15, driving 20 mph between the fields of tall corn, I thought, a one-car processional, and my mother, holding not a Bible on her lap, but the love poems of John Donne, which I imagined her reciting halfway out on the trestle where I had never been in the daylight and didn't want to be. And I was glad when Howard turned east by the landfill then circled back past the Carmelite Monastery where one of the nuns was on her knees in the grass, her hands not folded, but rather pressed flat against each other, fingers pointing toward the sky. "Steeple hands," my father had called them the night he showed me and Howard the different ways to pray.

I knew you could get to the river a lot of different ways, and this was one, though it was miles downstream from where we were supposed to be. Howard drove through a picnic area where there were a few green tables and a trash can and he continued past them down a bumpy two-track, and when he stopped and yanked on the emergency brake, we could see and hear the water.

"Here," Howard said, "this is where we did it," and I thought maybe it wasn't a lie if the ashes had drifted this far. It felt odd sitting there, nobody speaking, so I got out of the car and, in those polished black shoes and dress slacks, I walked through the goldenrod and thistle to the riverbank and stepped down to where the water had receded. I stooped, a kind of genuflection, and touched the water with the first two fingers of my right hand and, when I stood back up, I crossed myself. After a minute I opened my eyes and I could see Howard's wavy reflection beside me, and beside him, appearing like a ghost in black, my mother, her face so white when she lifted her veil. Howard crossed himself next, and he said aloud, "In the name of the Father, and of the Son," and my mother waited for him to finish, but he did not, and finally she said, "Amen."

I believe still that she was truly surprised when we all turned around and there was no one else there, just this congregation of three, and the Packard with both doors left open and the engine still running and the sun so bright on the windshield and windows that we had to shade our eyes. I remember exactly how Howard helped my mother step back up the bank in her high heels, and how, when she did, she kicked a penny loose from the soil at the highwater mark. I knew it couldn't be the penny I had thrown over the railing ten years earlier, but I picked it up anyway and squeezed it in one palm, squeezed it like a crucifix during the ride home while my mother, under her breath, recited John Donne, and Howard, his tie loosened now, was holding the steering wheel with both hands and already thinking beyond that day.

He did leave at the end of the summer, but not to a college town and not to find his natural mother and change his name. He hitchhiked north to Quebec, and from there, working his way on a freighter, to Europe. He sent us postcards from Amsterdam and Paris, and then a letter and a photo of him sitting at an outdoor cafe, his arm around some girl. He said he'd be back to see us soon but he didn't come, not for

two years, not until well after I'd gotten my driver's license
and drove alone one night to the railroad trestle, and sat
there, for I don't know how long. Until the river looked right,
I guess, the moon shimmering again on the water by the first
bend. And I threw the penny over and this time I did not wish
for a miracle. I didn't wish for anything. I was only sorry that
my mother had gotten, then lost, her job teaching literature
at the community college, and that the few small sand cherry
bushes I had found alive and transplanted from the nursery
looked so thin and scrawny in our front yard. I was sorry for a
lot of things I couldn't have changed, which I knew even then
was so stupid it was laughable. And I knew I'd be sorry again
when the guy who'd left the small deposit came by in the
morning to get the car. I had listened as my mother talked in
the driveway to the guy about it being a one-family car, a
good car. The guy said he didn't have a lot of money but that
he was nonetheless in the market for something reliable with
low miles and good tread on the tires. He started talking
about his wife and kids and I drifted off then and looked back
through the light drizzle toward the nursery and I could see
that a door to one of the outbuildings was open. It took only a
few minutes to walk out there. I didn't close the door, I
stepped inside the windowless shed and stared back out.
I listened to the guy start the car and let it idle and then I
watched him back it out and turn left and finally vanish
where the road curved into a decline. Then I watched my
mother standing there, her hands folded in front of her, and I
knew when she looked this way she couldn't see me. She
didn't take a single step toward the house or toward the
garage or toward the road. She just stood there confused. I
don't really know if I saw her lips move, or if I did, what it
was she said. All I heard was the rain coming down a little
harder. "God knows we need it," my father would have said,
opening his mouth to the clouds and telling us we'd been
blessed.

MISS DUNN

In fifth grade Miss Dunn did not arrange her seating by boy-girl, boy-girl, nor by alphabetical order. She placed us according to how dumb or smart we were. The dumbest kid was assigned to seat number one. That was Dwight Ironsides, and except for a few minutes one day, he never moved. Right next to him sat Gerald Boileau whose family had just uprooted to northern Michigan from Quebec. He arrived at the country school in November, two months after the school year had started. He spoke perfect French and he had a glass eye. Nobody in the class could tell it from the real one, though we speculated and argued, swearing to each other that we all had $20/20$ vision and really knew.

Gerald never slap-boxed or clowned around on the playground, and one cold morning Frank Sobota, without warning, shoved him hard against the galvanized fence behind the monkey bars, and announced to everyone watching that the eye was just an excuse to duck fights. Frank was the only kid I knew who used the big F word, and he kept calling Gerald a "fucking Frenchie," or sometimes a "chicken-shit foreigner." He held Gerald by the shirt front, ripping the first two buttons off, the loose cloth twisted into a fist he forced up under Gerald's chin. Frank was leaning close and staring into Gerald's green eyes, staring from one to the other. They matched perfectly.

"You *better* have a fake eye," Frank threatened, and then, wearing his brother's high school ring turned inward on his middle finger, he slapped Gerald on the side of the head, and Gerald raised one open hand, not in self-defense, but as the universal sign language of surrender.

"Fine, I'll prove it," Gerald said, and nodded when Frank let go and stepped a few feet back. Gerald waited, glanced at each of us and slowly took a new yellow pencil from one of those clear, plastic inserts that salesmen use to keep ink from staining their shirt pockets. Holding the pencil by the eraser end, he snapped open both eyes wider than I thought possible, and with the side of the sharpened lead he tapped the left one, the glass eye. "Okay?"

He was challenging Frank now, who answered, "Yeah, sure," and shrugged and seemed about to apologize when Gerald squeezed the glass eye shut and said, "I bet no one can make me blink!"

Art Baskin jabbed one finger just an inch from the good eye and we all laughed, a little nervous when Gerald didn't blink, the eye focusing somewhere beyond us, watery in the clear, cold light.

This test should have been enough to absolve him of cowardice or deceit. But he wanted more and, now that we had pushed him this far, he would give us the whole show. "Move closer," he whispered, "and watch this. Look way in."

He was not smiling when he lit a match and for a few long seconds held it so close to his glass eye we could see the round hardness, and in the black pupil the reflection of that single flame raging against the permanent darkness. I was glad when the bell rang, but before Gerald led us back to class, he straightened his shirt and zipped up his jacket and warned, "If Miss Dunn ever touches me . . . ," and without finishing he winked with his blind eye, the one that sometimes drifted shut when he read aloud from that front-row seat, giving those blind eye muscles a rest during the times his head was down, the sun slanting through the window like a sharp light he might have been shading, had he seen it on that half of his thin face, asleep above the open page.

His presentiment of Miss Dunn hitting him was the result of what had happened twice to Dwight Ironsides, twice in one day. She called on Dwight to solve a simple addition problem on the blackboard. He had been held back in both the first and third grades and was the biggest kid in the whole school, and clumsy, his red flocculent hair sticking up in an over-grown crew cut. His shoes were black and heavy, like factory shoes with steel toes, and he hardly lifted them when he walked. We all knew, as he picked up that new stick of chalk from the long easel, that he could not add 7 to 23. He would do okay combining the 7 and 3 on his fingers, but he would not know enough to carry the 1 to the next column. He would simply count to 10 and bring down the 2 so it looked like this:

$$\begin{array}{r} 23 \\ + \ 7 \\ \hline 210 \end{array}$$

Even the dummies in seats number three and four would raise their hands and wave them wildly, first one and, when it got tired, the other. Some kids would exaggerate their enthu-siasm with moans—ooo—oooooo—the painful anticipation of responding correctly for once, having figured such a sim-ple problem out in their heads. The students in the last three rows worked on independent projects during the dummie drills, but they would all peek when Miss Dunn snuck up behind Dwight and, gripping a social studies textbook in her hands, slam it down, whammo, right between his shoulder blades. He was never ready, never braced against the impact, the chalk always jarred loose in a kind of slow-motion loop to the black tiles where it busted into pieces. He rarely cried, and I never worried as much about him as I did about Gerald, wondering whether his glass eye would pop out from a blow like that, blind-sided and vicious. I even composed a note to Miss Dunn explaining this fear, but later crumpled it in the safe afternoon of that sacred back row.

It was Gerald's arrival that shifted me back with all the brains, right next to Carolyn Kruger who had won last week's spelling bee and was the only one who knew the capital of Idaho on the geography test. It was the extra credit question that no one could really study for. You knew it or you didn't. Gerald was escorted to the classroom by Mr. Boynton, the principal. He stood outside the door talking with Miss Dunn, and after a few minutes she brought Gerald in, introduced him, and ordered everyone but Dwight to get up and clean out their desks and move one seat to the right. Everyone clapped. The students like me who occupied the end seats advanced into another row. I smiled across the heads in front of me to where Miss Dunn was standing, her arms folded under her breasts, her dyed black hair just inches under the tip of the American flag. But when a few guys turned and smirked at me, I realized that I was the only boy back there. Not a single girl sat in the first row. Gerald thought he was given his seat because his last name began with a B. He said, "Thank you," and sat down and we all knew his turn at the blackboard was coming.

One morning before final bell Gerald asked Dwight, "How come you don't tell your parents?"

"I do. I've told them plenty of times, but they don't believe me. This is what they say—they say, 'Dwight, you were named after a president.' That's funny, isn't it? They say I don't learn because I don't listen good enough to Miss Dunn. I've gotta listen."

"You mean and just do nothing?"

"To pay attention," Dwight said, "even to things you don't understand."

"Negative capability," Gerald said, and I wondered how he knew a phrase like that.

"Huh, what?" Dwight asked.

"You and me are changing seats for the day."

"You won't like mine," Dwight said, shifting his gaze to the rest of us who felt a little strange kicking the new snow in front of us up the steps.

For almost an hour Miss Dunn pretended not to notice Gerald in Dwight's seat while we worked on penmanship. Gerald's was awful—he scribbled fast and small like a grownup. We passed all the papers forward to Gerald in Dwight's desk. Dwight had never passed his before and he held it tightly in two hands in front of him as though he were about to read from it, as though he had written a story. Even from the back row I could see the harsh, dark letters, the smudgy erasures, the end words cramped and curving below the blue lines. At first Dwight would not let go. He was used to hiding his paper in the middle of the stack, which he always straightened and handed to Miss Dunn. Already something was lost in the seat swap and, when Miss Dunn saw Dwight's paper on top she held it up by one corner as if it were a dirty sock, and dangled it in front of us, then lowered it to the level of Dwight's face.

"There's no name on this one," she said. "Would someone like to claim it?" No one did, not even Dwight. "Does anybody recognize the handwriting?" She needed no answer and, walking away, she said, "Dwight, go to the board and spell the name of the state in which Boston is the capital." A double question. I knew it, and instinctively raised my hand. So did Julie Novak, but it was Gerald, leaning back in Dwight's seat who piped up, "Massachusetts. M-A-S-S-A-C-H-U-S-E-T-T-S." As an afterthought he added, "Tea Party, Witch Trials, the Blue Laws." Outsiders always seemed to know more about our history than we did. Miss Dunn, turn-

ing then to face Gerald, did not ask, "Is your name Dwight?"
as she usually did when anyone answered out of turn, though
after the first week of school no one ever did. No one dared
slip like that. It meant a piece of masking tape across your
mouth. She was making her point, staring at Gerald and
calling him Dwight.

"Dwight, recite the first line of any English romantic
poem." Gerald responded again, without hesitation: "The
world is too much with us." He continued, both eyes closed,
his voiced mellifluous: "Little Mary Bell had a fairy in a nut."
He would have gone on but she cut him short, changing the
subject.

"Dwight, whose face is on the hundred-dollar bill?" She
knew his family was poor, that his father had moved here to
take a job at Pet Ritz where all day he lifted damaged pies
from the conveyor belt. She was sure Gerald had never seen a
hundred-dollar bill, but he knew.

"Ben Franklin," he said, as though he knew him personally.
"He wanted the wild turkey as the national symbol instead of
the bald eagle." Was he testing her now? Later I looked that
up and it was true.

"Dwight, how many eyes does a flounder have on the same
side of its head?"

"Two eyes," Gerald said, but he was quiet now, tentative.
"Both on one side, Picasso-like."

So she knew, and whatever Gerald might have had planned
to shock her with his glass eye would fall flat. She'd just grab
him calmly by his long arm and jerk him out of Dwight's seat
and drag him to the principal's office. He'd return alone after
a half hour, his knuckles red from the ruler, and maybe he'd
be crying as he crossed in front of us to seat number two.
They had ways of making you behave. But we all knew now
that Gerald was even smarter than Ann Johnson who sat in
the last seat in the last row. There was an extra desk next to
her where Miss Dunn sat and corrected arithmetic tests once
a week for that hour the art teacher came in to take over the
class. Miss Dunn's black sweater was still draped over the

back of the chair and, when she made Gerald stay late after school that day, that's where he sat, alone in the room, writing "Dwight Ironsides" five hundred times.

When he finished he left the paper and pencil right there and came out the side door, shaking his cramped fingers. I was waiting for him in the cold with Frank. As soon as Gerald spotted us he packed a snowball and flung it hard against the old bricks. Frank thought that was his signal and started in: "That fucking witch," and there she was staring down from the lighted, second-floor window, and her lips seemed very red behind the wavy glass to the two of us who saw her, glancing back as we followed Gerald who moved away after Thanksgiving, and the rows moved back to fill that space.

LAND TIDES

My father's name is Warren James Pendergast. I'm not sure what I'm giving away when I say this story is not about his arrest, though I know it's impossible to completely ignore an event like that. So I won't. But believe me, I've since learned that there are much worse things to endure in this life than a short prison term. There are things that happen that can break a person's heart.

But it's still a few minutes before the actual beginning of any of that. It's Friday, around noontime, and Warren is out on bail after hurting a man from Camp Grayling, a man in uniform in the parking lot of Captain Jack's, a real dive, Warren says, where the hard-calved topless dancers are all underaged. I don't know why he goes there, nor what the fight was about this time, nor how much money Lillian, his girlfriend of five years, has had to borrow. Probably a lot, by the way she's saying nothing and chain-smoking and driving so fast, the front end of the pickup shimmying like crazy, the tires whining. Warren is always careful behind the wheel. At least he is when I'm in the truck. That's one way he's a responsible father. I guess he never forgets that his dad was the victim of a hit-and-run.

"How about if you slow down just a hair," Warren says as we pass the BP gas and Battalion II Bingo and Louis's Wholesale Meats on Route 12, keeping pace with the heavier traffic moving parallel to us up on the interstate. He says, "Remember, these plates are expired."

"Yeah," Lillian says, "like a lot of things around here lately." Meaning Warren's job, for starters. He's down to two days a week, installing carpeting. He claims most everybody up here is dead-assed out of options and unemployment checks. Maybe that's just an alibi for spending too much time in the bars. And for late nights of low-stake poker. Lillian says it is. She's kept up her end during the school year by substitute teaching at the junior high. Seems kind of screwy that the two of them would hook up like this, but I'm glad they did. Her degree is in French. You should hear how fluent she is when she speaks it. And how sexy it sounds. I'm here because it's mid-July, the month I come to visit. It's not exactly tradition yet—it's only my second time. But if it's still possible, I want to get to know my dad before I grow up, like he never had the chance with his. I want a normal life.

Lillian keeps the accelerator pressed down hard, like this time she doesn't care if they're on a collision course that could ruin for good what they've got going together. I've never seen her so upset.

I've heard them argue before, seesawing back and forth, but never like this. This time I'm squeezed in between them in the cab, a Plymouth Powerwagon with a rollbar and a missing tailgate and the windshield cracked all the way across at eye-level by a single B.B. There's a ton of heat blowing up from somewhere underneath the dashboard, right onto my legs, and we're all sweltering and drenched in sweat.

Even so, Lillian smells good, but not Warren. He smells like someone who's been sick in bed with a high fever. That mixed with old Aqua Velva. So I'm leaning a little toward her. When she catches my eye in the rearview mirror she says, "Here, pass these over."

They're color slides. Warren holds them up to the windshield, studying them right through the glassine envelopes. Like maybe they're slides from a wedding or a trip to Mammouth Cave where he promised to take me last year but never did. He says that trip is still on the back burner. Someday I imagine we'll go.

It was Lillian who snapped the entire roll early this morning with her Instamatic and had them developed a few hours later at Picture Quick while we waited. All twenty-four are shots of the mobile home, each from a slightly different angle.

"Any in particular you like more than the others?" she says, like she's planning to have enlargements printed up and framed for the relatives so she can show off what she and Warren have made of their lives. They've got new aquamarine skirting around the base of the trailer, and wisteria where I've seen humming birds.

Warren gets the point she's making—it's her house that she's put up for collateral, it's her name on the deed. He's learned something from his marriage to my mom—he's learned to stay calm with a women in situations like this that could blow sky high. He's learned, when he's in domestic trouble, how not to yell.

"This one," he says after a while, and I lean forward to see which he's chosen. It's one of the ones taken from the backside of the property, so the new deck is in clear view, and the two aluminum lawn chairs and, off to the side, an oil drum where he burns the trash. If you squint hard, you can make out a foot dangling a red flip-flop out the partially opened screen door. It's my foot. I might even be smiling because, until now, everything seemed good at their place. It's not like at home where I have my own bedroom and window fan and shelves of model planes and aircraft carriers. That's my hobby, building war models. But I sleep okay here on the fold-out sofa, especially if there's a breeze and if Warren's not snoring too loud.

It's the arrangement he and my mom have worked out, though she wishes I didn't want to visit him. Not ever. But he's my father, so where's the argument? Nowhere, and she knows it. She'd just rather I attended space camp in Texas, which is what kids around the country like me who are serious about becoming astronauts do every summer. I've been once, and it's fun. Warren joked with me that landing in northern Michigan was probably quite a bit like landing on the moon. Or on Mars. Just a different set of bearings, he said. Just another remote patch of dead land to put down on.

I was five or six when my mom left him for good, and we moved back to Boulder Junction, Wisconsin, which is where she's from and where she took up again with an old boyfriend named Dwayne Chance, a nobody in my book, which means he didn't figure long in our lives and, when that went sour, she stayed away from men. She's not a feminist or anything like that. She's a hairstylist with her own beauty nook in our basement, and she can still turn a few heads. She's pretty. One of the first questions Warren always asks me when I get off the Greyhound, before we even get reacquainted, is who she's seeing these days. I don't have to lie to him. I say, "Nobody, that's who."

I'm glad we're not crammed into a trailer court where, like some friends of mine, you always hear somebody telling somebody else to lower his voice. Or where you can see the hazy, bluish light of the TVs at night clouding the windows when you're out walking or driving slowly past to your own crowded shirttail of a lot. We're off by ourselves in the country, off River Road, so Lillian doesn't wear much when she sunbathes. I'm fourteen, and it feels good when she squeezes a gunky line of Coppertone between my shoulder blades, then rubs it all over my back and arms and neck. Warren hardly ever takes off his shirt outside because he burns so badly. And then he blisters. Lillian says it's too bad because he looks like Charles Atlas. He looks like you want to look on a crowded beach. Maybe that's how he ended up with a younger woman.

Lillian will be twenty-seven next week. Sometimes she unstraps her bikini top and lies facedown on the oversized towel, elbows out, her head resting on the backs of her hands. I can see the bulge of her breasts from the side when I walk by, which I do frequently. Like lots of people from the Midwest, she's no Esther Williams—that's what Warren says. The fact is, she can't swim a stroke. But she loves the water on days like this with high humidity and temperatures in the nineties. Scorchers. Today's proof-positive that we get our fair share, even this far north.

That's why Warren hauled in those two old bathtubs last summer, the deep-bellied kind with the lion's feet, and placed them side by side on the parched lawn. The only green is where they drain. Warren calls them affordable dual pools. No filters to clean, no measuring cups of chlorine to dump in. Each pool has a hard, white rubber stopper on a chain. That's it. And no faucets, so you can lean right back at either end, depending on the direction of the sun. It takes less than half an hour to fill them both to the top with the hose. And take it from me, you cool off in a hurry once you squat on your haunches, and then let go of the sides and take the plunge.

And that's what's on everyone's mind today, cooling off. Bodies and tempers. Lillian has parked the pickup in the shade under the huge oak, next to her busted down VW bus. Warren says it needs a water pump, but he hasn't been able to locate one from the junkyards. Not yet. The part new is too expensive, so the bus sits. But not up on blocks, as Warren points out. He's not the kind of low life who tows junkheaps in and pops the hoods and leaves them there to rust. If he were, Lillian explained to me, he sure wouldn't be living with a woman who's been to Paris.

She's in their bedroom changing out of her blouse and skirt, and Warren, decked-out in his Jockey shorts and T-shirt, has already disappeared up to his neck in the tub that says "HIS," spray-painted in black letters across the ivory porcelain. The other tub is still filling. It says "HERS." There's a board across each. On Warren's, a sweating bottle of Pabst Blue Ribbon and a pack of Old Golds and a .44 caliber Smith and Wesson— the essentials, he says, to survive the afternoon.

It always makes Warren groggy when he drinks in the hot sun. Then he gets even quieter. The gun doesn't frighten me though—I've fired it lots of times at rats at the dump. Or at bottles or aerosol cans, anything that will shatter or pop in the dusky, final, flat gray light of any evening. We pass Camp Grayling on our way there, and Warren slows down so I can see the rows of tanks and sometimes soldiers in the turrets. The pickup's radio always crackles, fading in and out on that stretch of road. Warren says it's the military radar screwing up the airways. I wish I could watch the tanks on maneuvers. Right now artillery shells from the training field are exploding in distant bursts behind us like thunder.

But there's no storm approaching. This day is moored under a stationary blue sky, the clouds all burned away and no breeze whatsoever. A day to conserve. I'm gulping ice water, and even my palm on the cold glass is sticky. I'm about to go outside too and take a dip.

"Guy," Warren yells inside to me. "S'il vous plâit, my lighter when you come out." He must have learned that from Lillian.

"Here it is," she says, sliding it into that little slit of a pocket right below the elastic band of my bathing trunks. It's a gold-plated Ronson with his initials, WJP, engraved on both sides, the last anniversary present he got from my mom. Lillian has walked quietly into the stuffy kitchen where I've been standing at the sink and staring out the window at Warren soaking like a seal, his head back, eyes closed. Lillian is wearing only a half-slip and bra and, inside, my stomach has started to go all weird. It's not the first time either. If Warren wasn't so close by, I'd say she was coming on to me.

"Oh, hi," which is all I can muster, your basic dumbo response to a woman who's standing close to you in her silk undergarments and holding what's left of a cigarette by the recessed filter. A Parliament.

"Excusez-moi," she says, pressing the chrome pedal of the wastebasket with her bare foot. The top lifts smoothly, the way I can never make it do, and she drops her cigarette butt inside. Her toenails are polished pink, and her hair is combed back into a ponytail. Age-wise, we're almost as close as she is to Warren. He's thirty-nine. And we're both thin and about the same height, 5'6".

Making it possible for the two of us to squeeze into one bathtub, though we've never done this before and I sure wouldn't be the one to suggest it. But Warren does. He says it's just too hot to take turns. "Good God Almighty," he says, "you can taste the air," and he licks his lips and raises his beer and takes, as he says, "One giant sip for mankind." He winks at me then, the first sign from him so far that things are going to simmer down and be all right.

But I'm worried for him. I wish he'd keep joking—I dread these long waves of silence. I can tell what's surfacing in each of our minds is the bad trouble he's in. And it's eerie the way nobody's talking, like what he did last night is some big secret they need to keep hidden from me. Or from each other. It's like they've fallen asleep, nothing moving except for the surface water I move around with a kind of slow motion breast-stroke when it gets too warm, the ripples lapping against Lillian's chin and neck. She's been holding onto both my ankles and tightening her grip every now and then, the way you do sometimes twitching in a dream. And her legs are spread apart on top of mine and it's a soft and strange and oblong light that wavers underwater across the smooth insides of her thighs.

II

We're a thousand miles from any ocean, but I'm imagining the moon and the tides and, when Lillian steps outside onto the deck, that it's a raft we're standing on, and that the dual pools are buoys out there bobbing in the dark, and that the water is low enough finally for us to wade out and maybe hold onto them and talk.

"Can't sleep?" she asks, and I shake my head. "No," I say, "not all that good," and she says back, "I know, me either." Warren, however, is inside snoring away hard-core.

"Seems pretty calm," I say, but Lillian thinks I mean the water, and she lifts her nightgown right over her head and she's wearing nothing underneath and I stare at her bug-eyed because I've never once in my entire life been skinny-dipping with a woman.

I'm almost certain I'll hear a splash when she steps from the stair, or her sloshing out ahead of me, but of course I don't. And then I think, Land tides. Even if there is no water, there's this powerful undertow, and I'm naked too and being carried farther and farther away from the house trailer that seems to be rocking back and forth behind us. Warren, reading in the newspaper about a local drowning, is the one who told me never to struggle against a current, so I don't. I surrender to it instead, though I know this is not what he meant and, already, I sense the danger I'm in.

Only one of the pools is full and the water warm, right down to the bottom, which is good this late at night because it's cool out and Lillian says, "Come on in," and I do, facing her and the trailer and I'm certain this time that I've already committed a crime, if that's what an erection that aches is in this situation, here in midsummer in a dark bathtub, just me and my father's girlfriend, alone in the middle of the backyard surrounded by pines. And fireflies. And the high frequency songs of crickets. And maybe I shouldn't admit it to myself, but part of me is glad I'm not at space camp where, in the fake cockpit of an Apollo rocket, the simulated blast-offs and orbits of distant galaxies could never make me feel the excitement I'm feeling here beneath this actual universe of northern stars.

"Are you a nighttime navigator, Guy?" she asks, and she's staring up, as if from the hull of a boat, as if the two of us are drifting without oars or sails away from the shore, way out into some exotic lagoon. Maybe somewhere off the coast of France.

"You mean like in dreams?" I say, and Lillian says, "I suppose. Yes, partly that. Voyages that take you for a little while away from all this."

She hasn't used the word sex, but she's leaning toward me and, as she does, Warren steps out onto the deck—I actually hear the clink of his lighter before I see him and, as the cigarette catches, I glimpse his face behind the flame, then him bending slowly to pick up my pajama bottoms and Lillian's nightgown.

Although I'm sure he can't see us, he knows where we've disappeared to, and all he can do now is wait and hope that we'll return before we go too far. But we already have.

"The truth," Lillian says, "is that Warren is a violent man, and that's why I never married him. Do you know what marriage is, do you, Guy? It's the privilege and the promise to become a little happier than what you already are. That's my definition. It means children and family, and look what kind of a father Warren has been."

"He's behind you," I whisper, "he's standing on the deck." But at that moment the back door hesitates on its swing-hinge, and then it closes.

Lillian is not alarmed. She says simply that it's over between them, that it has been and now, after what we've done, he knows it too. "There's no future with him," she says. And she says also that he'll go to jail this time and that he deserves this punishment, meaning us turning on him, which I never intended to do but have. I believe he loves me and Lillian too and that he'll take no revenge. "Things end," she says. "It's the world."

And next, the unavoidable—she kisses me on the mouth. Then I let her do what she does to me with her hand. When I stand up a few minutes later, I begin to shiver badly in the breeze.

"Blame me," Lillian says, "and I'll blame it on desire and despair." And even though I don't understand what that means, I nod. I say, "Okay." But almost nothing is. I offer to go get us each a towel, and she says, "Yes, please." She says, "Merci."

Warren would call what moon there is tonight a pathetic moon, meaning there's almost no light. Except in the bedroom where he's rummaging through his belongings. I've stopped halfway between the house and the dual pools. All night I've heard helicopters taking off and coming back to Camp Grayling, and there's one above me now, much closer than they've been. I imagine its search-beam flooding the backyard and blinding me and someone shouting through a megaphone for me to lie down on my stomach and clasp my hands behind my head. And that's what I do.

But I realize too that this is where the fantasy ends. There will be no spectacular capture. I'll simply get up in a little while when I've stopped crying, and get a couple of towels from the bathroom like I said I would. And then get packed and, in the morning, board the Greyhound and go scot-free across state lines to Wisconsin where my mom will meet me at the Boulder Junction depot, glad that I've wised-up and escaped that nothing existence Warren and his young girl-friend live. And Lillian will stay right here because, as she made perfectly clear, the property and the mobile home are in her name on the deed. And Warren? I believe that he won't jump bail. He'll show up for the trial and be convicted, without the protest of decent council, of assault and begin serving his thirty days. The vision I have is of him being led from the courthouse in handcuffs—that's often the case when the law gets all over a man who's made too many mistakes in a small town.

If that man turns out to be your father, you're obliged to come to his defense. Even if that only means to curl up the circular and tap it for a few minutes on the mailbox because nothing else is there. No letter from him, no postcard. Not yet. Which also means no return address for you to get hold of him, in case you're ever in trouble, the way sons end up sometimes without their fathers, who, even after years and years go by, they want back.

KILLING TIME

Paul Burkholder always had firecrackers, and sitting on my back porch again he kept lighting inchers, one after another, holding then tossing each over the railing where they exploded, the shreds of blue-and-red paper settling on the shiny green leaves of pachysandra. Jimmy Sterzic was there too, as always, chewing squares of bubble gum and reading the Bazooka Joe comics and laughing like a nut.

My father wasn't crazy about us hanging around all day but there was nothing else to do, which was exactly what I said to him one afternoon in July when he got home from work at the plant, like he was somehow to blame for our boredom, and he said back, slowly and sounding exhausted, "You'll all three end up in the service someday and it'll be the best thing ever happened. Someday, and they'll straighten you out good."

But we weren't scared of going, not at fourteen we weren't, and when my father walked inside, the screen door slamming behind him, Paul Burkholder said quietly, "I'd enlist in a minute if they'd let me. The army'd be cool. Artillery or demolition. Shit, just blow stuff up all day."

Jimmy, taking the pink wad of gum out of his mouth, lobbed it hand-grenade style over the unmown lawn, and when it hit, he said, kind of in slow motion, "Kaaaboooom."

My father had told me once how he lied about his age so he could go fight in Europe during WW II. But there was no war now and we weren't going anywhere, not without a driver's license or a set of wheels. Paul was just talking big and I said to him, "You'd hate taking orders, you'd hate it."

"No worse than rotting here," Paul said, "in East Bumfuck, Egypt," and Jimmy chimed in, "You got that right," and he reached for one of Paul's Old Golds from the new pack between them on the gray floorboards. Paul stole four, sometimes five packs a week from his mother's cartons in their pantry. We all knew she drank like a fish and, as Paul would say when he was mad at her, she smoked like a chimney, too. Booze and tobacco. Paul said one time that she was worse than a reservation Indian, but he got real sad when he said that and, I guess to make a joke out of it, he said, "Watch this," and he put the lit end of his cigarette into his mouth and closed his lips and bellowed his cheeks, blowing the smoke out backwards. Then he put a finger in each ear and opened his eyes wide and blew some more until his face turned beet red and he fell to the ground, pretending to pass out. "That's my old lady," he said, spitting out the cigarette. "A drunken Indian smokestack."

Paul almost never burned himself doing stunts like that, and already the first two fingers on his right hand were stained with nicotine. He smoked in the boy's room at school and on the back of the bus, cupping his cigarette behind the seat in front of him and exhaling out the half-opened window.

But it wasn't a cigarette he put between his lips this afternoon—it was an incher and I didn't like him fooling around like that and I said so.

"Come on, how much?" he asked. "Put your money where your mouth is."

"Your mouth," I said.

"Five bucks!" Jimmy said. "Five big ones if you light it," and he took a long drag and flicked the ash on the stairs and handed Paul the cancer stick.

I shook my head and said, "You'll look great without a face," remembering how he'd bitten down hard on a ladyfinger one night and lit it and how, when it went off, it sounded dull and small but left wicked powder burns on his front teeth and scorched his gums so he couldn't hardly eat for almost a week. An incher had ten times the wallop, so I figured he'd never really do it, but he did, touching the fuse alive and closing his eyes. I yelled out, "Spit it out, Jesus God," and jumped off the stairs, Jimmy right behind me and ducking to one side.

When the sparks died, Jimmy straightened and took one step forward and said, "Holy shitburger, a goddamned dud," but we moved no closer, not until Paul opened his eyes and I eased the incher out and dropped it quick and ground it back and forth under my sneaker. I said, "You're mental, you know that?" and all he said was, "Yeah, I know," and all that evening, feeding small sticks to a campfire in the backyard, we discussed how he'd beaten the odds, fifty, maybe seventy-five to one.

"You bet your ass," Paul said. "Now let's risk ourselves to something big, something we'll be remembered by."

"Such as?" Jimmy asked, and Paul said, still staring into the flames, "Such as snuffing out this hick shittown." He blew three perfect smoke rings above the fire.

"You got a bomb now I suppose?" Jimmy said. "Or a mortar launcher?" and he laughed until Paul looked up at him and then over at me and he said, "No, with our thumbnails. We'll obliterate this whole place with no more than our thumbnails," and he stood and reached his fist above his head, his thumb sticking up, and he covered up the full moon, and then Venus and then all of Orion's belt. "All you need is distance. Try it," he said, and we did, the three of us standing close together and saying nothing, ready this time to leave our mark on the world.

None of us had ever climbed the water tower and we didn't know anyone who had, though the town's old population, 5,442, was painted in huge white letters across all that green. But since the copper mines had failed, maybe there were half that many people and most everyone was out of work. Paul said he bet those numbers were at least fifteen feet high and Jimmy said, "Horseshit," and then a second time when I swore I could see the tower swaying just a fraction against the blue sky. "In a strong wind it might, sure," Paul said, but it was real still that morning where we were standing, me and Paul craning our necks and shading our eyes while Jimmy recoiled the rope and threw it up again and this time the heavy knot on the end went through the first ladder rung far enough for me to jump up and grab it and pull it down. Then Jimmy, working from his knees, tied a slip noose and snugged up the slack and tested the rope by hanging on it with his full weight.

"Be my guest," he said, and I spit on my palms and started up, hand over hand, just like I'd done in gym one day, a few girls whispering and watching me from the fold-out bleachers. I made it all the way to the ceiling, the only one to ever have touched it, according to Mr. Nykerk who'd taught phys ed in Ludlow for nineteen years. I remember how I never once peeked down and how I had yelled, suspended between those steel rafters, for someone to drag the mats away so it would seem more dangerous. I could hear Mr. Nykerk say, "No," to the other boys. "No," he said, and later Paul told me how Mr. Nykerk had motioned them all to move away and how he piled mats on top of one another, the whole time staring up like he expected me to jump. "Dumb," was all he said to me when I got down, "dumb, dumb, dumb." But a few weeks later, sitting with my father at a parent-teacher conference, Mr. Nykerk referred to me as a regular Jack-in-the-Beanstalk. "Nonsense," my father had said, "my boy's scared to death of heights," but I said no, I wasn't anymore, that I'd conquered that fear, and I nodded at him lots of times and Mr. Nykerk did, too, my father looking back and forth between us, saying finally that it was smarter to turn away from what frightened us. Like he had at sixteen, walking out of a mine shaft his first day down. "Chicken shit," some of the guys had called at him, "asshole," but they weren't saying anything now, he said, those who stayed to raise their kids on welfare checks or, like Paul's dad, had driven away alone late one night and never returned. "Fear is where you don't belong," my father had lectured, but I was climbing again, thinking, what did he know, slaving away in some hole-in-the-wall factory that made sun visors for GM. Like Paul had said the night before, we needed distance, and no place loomed higher than the water tower, and if I got scared halfway up I wasn't turning around. I carried a jackknife in the back pocket of my dungarees, and I'd at least scratch my initials on top, and the year, 1959. Beyond that, there wasn't a plan, not yet, or a way of seeing much beyond my fingers which squeezed the first iron rung and then the next and the next, Paul and Jimmy screaming for me to slow down.

Sweating pretty bad, I wondered if there really was water up there and a way to dive in and if the water was real cold inside all that steel, cold like an ocean. I imagined the three of us swimming naked some muggy night then, side by side, hitching our elbows over the edge of the tower and sharing an Old Gold and watching the lights of houses blink on and off like distant boats. And I thought how we really could obliterate this hick town with our thumbnails—my factory father who always played it safe and gave out too much advice, and Paul's drunken mother, and Jimmy's oldest sister who we knew rejected her family and whored around in the bars, not that she was wrong exactly, but all those people we loved made us awful edgy doing what they did with their lives. So, no matter the danger, we'd rise above them, literally.

"Move it," I yelled down to Paul and Jimmy, and suddenly the half summer we had left felt like too little time, and I started climbing again, my heart pounding and pounding in a way that had nothing to do with heights.

The three of us sat with our backs against the tower, right under the huge white numbers. A stiff breeze blew out of the north behind us, and Jimmy, looking pale, said, "Damn if this thing ain't moving," and he pulled his knees tight to his chest and spread his fingers wide and placed his palms carefully on the floor of the catwalk as if for balance and he wouldn't move them, not even when Paul offered him a smoke. "Take one," Paul said, "come on," but Jimmy just shook his head no and straightened his spine and pressed his head back and closed his eyes.

"Christ," he said, "we're so goddamn high," and I thought for a minute that he might panic, but he didn't, and when I got up to circle counterclockwise around the tower, he said, "Mother of God." He said, "Dougie, be fucking careful," and he flinched when I stepped by him and said, "Hey, we're on a roll, remember? We're just raising the stakes a little. It's duck soup. We can't lose."

"Yes we can," he said. "Me and Paul, we wiggled the powder out. We ain't on a roll, Dougie. That incher wasn't really a dud."

Paul took a long, deep drag on his cigarette and shrugged at me like, what the hell, we're here, right?, and we're not bored out of our skulls for once, but he seemed awful nervous too, as he flicked his butt away from his lips, flicked it way out and we both watched it, not so much dropping as floating sideways, as though on the surface of a perfectly clear river, a few giant boulders on the bottom glaring up from over a hundred feet below.

From the back side of the tower I could see the town dump, the thin smoke rising, and I could hear the blunt barking of Roy Magoon's Airedale and the intermittent pop of a .22, and I wished right then that I had my father's spotting scope so I could make out who it was was shooting. Probably Roy himself who rarely left and always scrunched up his eyebrows, like he was surprised whenever you asked if you could hunt the rats too. He'd let you, no problem, but he just liked to be asked. Most guys who came, came just before dark, some with handguns, like Jimmy's dad, and some after dark, their engines idling, and they'd sit on the hoods of their cars or pickups, drinking quarts of beer and taking aim down the steady beam of headlights.

My father called it "killing time," meaning it both ways, like it was time to kill and also that it passed the dead hours when there was nothing else for folks to do. He didn't want me going there and I didn't go much, except to drive over with him each Saturday morning to dump our garbage. He'd back up the station wagon and I'd get out and open the rear door and heave the bags over the edge onto the main pile. Sometimes I'd kind of whip the bags so they broke open, the contents spraying all over. My father, watching through the rearview mirror, wouldn't say anything, saving the silence, I guess, so that when he did speak it was supposed to carry more clout. But it didn't. On the way out he'd say the same thing every time he saw Roy Magoon asleep on a battered recliner in the dump shack. He'd say, "Some existence," and I'd nod, pretending to agree, but I figured Roy was a natural to the symmetry of this county as anyone else who chose to stay and wait things out, scavenging to stay alive if that's what it took until times changed.

Which they never did, so the population decreased every year. People dying or leaving and nobody new coming in, except for the Sellgrins. I never knew why they moved up here. What I did know was that Phyllis Sellgrin was the most seductive girl I'd ever seen, a tenth grader who gave me this godawful feeling in my stomach whenever she'd pass me in the halls, ignoring me like I didn't exist. Paul, one day holding a cherry bomb between his thumb and finger, said it reminded him of a giant nipple. "Like Phyllis Sellgrin's nipples," he said and I said back, "Keep dreaming," and we both laughed and traded punches on the arm, shoving each other as we ran, bent over, away from the half-filled can of paint which exploded behind us. We walked back to check the damage, and Paul, starting one of our standard jokes, said, "How they hanging?" and I said, "Same as always—round and firm and full of sperm."

"Ditto," he said and we pointed out to each other how the undersides of the maple leaves had turned sticky red and dripping almost twenty feet up.

"Some nipple," I said.

"Yeah," Paul said, "I'd sure as hell think twice about sticking that one in my mouth."

But I wouldn't have, not on my life. She was one in a million, which were about the odds of me ever getting closer to her than fantasy. But I liked even that much, up here with the fat clouds passing and the breeze on my face and the sound of a semi gearing down for the junction of 28 and 41, probably heading east to Marquette or Escanaba. I wondered, if at night I could solve the puzzle of streets and houses, and if, through the scope, I could glimpse Phyllis crossing her bedroom, maybe in just a white slip, or see her pause, staring out the window at the stars before pulling the shade and killing the lights.

This was the place to be, okay, an outpost, and if Paul and Jimmy could get their minds off falling I believed we'd all be saved. I almost wished my father was below me so I could hang right over and shout down to him that I wasn't afraid, that I'd beaten that fear just like I said. It was easy. In your gut you simply had to believe you couldn't die. Not like Jimmy who was terrified and who, right that minute, was calling me, "Dougie." And then his voice higher pitched, "Dougie," and then Paul's voice, too, "Come on, Dougie, dont't fuck around," and I kicked off one of my sneakers, then the other one, and watched them for almost a full minute tumble end over end and when they hit the ground they bounced, who knows how far, in opposite directions, and I yelled back to those guys, "Okay, let's get down," which we all did, safe and sound, and we peddled our bikes hard to my backyard and leaned them against the side of the house where they stayed all afternoon while we talked and smoked until my father came home and stepped slowly between us up the stairs, pausing and saying nothing and touching my head in a way he hadn't done for months. Then he turned and bummed a cigarette off Paul and he even sat down with us and poured himself a cup of muddy coffee from his thermos, but he didn't drink more than a sip. "Terrible," he said, and emptied the rest onto the lawn. He make-believe shivered to show his distaste, but it was Friday and very warm still and I knew he'd sweat doing a little yardwork, maybe spading under the honeysuckle, and after that he'd turn on the sprinkler and have a slow beer and take a shower and get ready to watch the fights on TV. "Club fighters, has-beens," he'd say without fail, "every last one of them punchdrunk." But he'd be right there watching every round, bobbing and weaving on the edge of the couch as though he were the one getting clobbered. Sometimes he'd shout instructions: "Get out of there, stay the hell away," like the only intelligent strategy was to run for ten rounds, even if you lost and got booed. At least you'd be around to collect on another payday. "Marciano or Dempsy could have licked the whole bunch on the same night," he'd say. "Or Jake Lamada." But he wasn't talking boxing just then, though he did hit me on the cheek with a light, open-handed left, and I covered up, my fists in front of my face, and Paul and Jimmy, they kind of laughed, my father winking at them before he stood up and walked away, his thermos under his arm, the same black lunchpail he'd carried for years and years swinging at his side.

"Stay down, you bum," my father kept yelling to the white guy who'd hit the canvas for a second time. "Stay down for Christsake." The crowd at ringside was on its feet, the referee counting, "seven, eight, nine," and I closed the front door quietly behind me.

Paul was waiting at the end of the driveway, the tip of his cigarette glowing orange as he took a drag. "Here," he said, taking a few steps forward, and he handed me a single Roman candle, the last one he had left.

"I'll watch from the river," he said, and I said, "Okay, good," and I checked to see if I had the new book of matches in the army knapsack, which I did, along with my father's scope and a single bottle of beer and an opener.

"Don't drink that up there," he said. "I'm telling you, drunks have shitty balance. Check out my mother's eye," he said, "from her last fall."

In the distance we both watched a flash of heat lightning, which Paul mistook for a storm heading our way.

"Nonsense," I said. "Look at the stars," and he held up his thumbnail in front of his one open eye and said, "What stars?" and I said, "You sure you won't come?" and he said, without any hesitation, "Forget it, once is plenty for me."

Jimmy wanted no part of this either, and he'd gone to the dump with his dad instead, and his dad's friend, a guy named Webster Crockett. People called him Davey because he shot so good, but he'd had a seizure at the dump one night and scared hell out of everyone, squeezing his pistol so hard nobody could pry it loose from his hand. An ambulance arrived finally from Nagaunee, and Jimmy, who was there the whole time, said he'd never seen anything so eerie, that white ambulance and the red light flashing across all that garbage and across Webster's contorted face and nobody shooting rats except for Roy Magoon who kept saying, "Let him lay a while, he'll be fine. Just give him some air goddamnit." And

Webster was fine after that, if he'd take his medication, but still he always made Jimmy mighty nervous. "Then don't go," I said to him, but anything was preferable to the water tower, even if it meant sighting down a gun barrel right next to Webster Crockett, who'd tell you, "Squeeze the trigger," to whoever was shooting next to him and flinching. "Squeeze," he'd say, "like you love 'er, like this," and he'd take careful aim, his hand perfectly steady, and when a rat crawled into range, he'd pop it every time.

So I was going it alone. I caught a glimpse of Paul's face in the headlights of a passing car, and his face looked like a death mask, white and pasty, which spooked me, and I said, "What the hell you doing?" and he said, "What? I'm not doing anything." But he was, acting scared, abandoning the one real chance we had to steal this night, soar above this crippled town.

I wanted to tell him he was chicken-shit spineless, all talk and no action, and that the world really would be different up there if he'd only relax, and that even one slow orbit around the tower might change his life, the way mountain climbers said it did them, reaching the summit of Mount McKinley or Mount Everest, then just sitting and staring out at night. But feeling lonely, too, I figured, which was all part of it, renewing, momentarily, an interest in death. Which is the reverse of what my father said. "Keep clear of it," he said. "Mr. Death arrives on his own soon enough."

"Ask the rats," I said to Paul, who said, "The rats? What rats?" and he shook his head and said, "You're looney sometimes," and he got on his bike and glided across the road, then back to my side farther down, his generator light glowing redder and redder the faster he pedaled, and I shouted after him, "Fucker," and I'm sure he flipped me the bird, the way he would at his own house some nights, having argued with his mother who, at those times, he said he hated.

"You don't hate her, not really," I'd say and he'd answer every time, "You don't know, Dougie, not about this subject you don't," which maybe was true, and I thought about my mother who'd been dead almost ten years and how Paul could be a king dork saying the things he did, calling his mother a drunken Indian Smokestack in front of us, dumb stuff like that. My father said booze was poison to all Indians, even if they were only a quarter blood, like Mrs. Burkholder, whose grandfather was Ottawa, a chief, Paul told people, but no one except me ever really believed him.

Earlier in the summer he'd stolen a six-pack of Pabst Blue Ribbon from home, and me and him and Jimmy each drank two beers while sitting on the flat rocks under the bridge, telling jokes and toasting the cars that passed, the tires slapping above us over the loose boards. Paul got the most looped, so maybe that part of the Indian still was in him. Jimmy was feeling pretty good, too, though, and he stood up and smashed his empties, one right after the other, against the abutment on the far side of the river and he laughed and reached then for Paul's empties and Paul said, "Hey, back off." He looked at both of us like he was mad, but he smiled right away and pressed the bottle caps back on with the heel of his hand and tossed the two bottles underhanded a little ways up the river. They bobbed, then tipped sideways. Paul had already tied a rock to an M-80 which he lit and we watched it sink for a few seconds before we ducked back and covered up, the waterproof fuse spitting pink and white. When it exploded, there was almost no sound, but both bottles busted into a million brown slivers around us. "Yeah," Paul had shouted. "Yeah, yeah, yeah," his war cry against boredom, and Jimmy, all crazy now too, yelled, "More firewater, more goddamn firewater for us savages," and he whooped and whooped but I said nothing, all wet now and still nursing my second beer and watching a few big suckers float belly-up in front of me, their tails twitching as they tried to right themselves, the slow current carrying them into the moonlight.

Always something dying in this town for fun, and that's what I kept thinking as I climbed the water tower, about that and suicide, which Paul said earlier was the only reason anyone fell in love with heights. "You go up there and like it," he said, "then part of you wants to jump."

"Or fly," I whispered to myself, and I could hear the rumble of thunder way off and the wind kicking up in the tops of the trees and the temperature dropping, the way it does sometimes right before a downpour. But I felt only a few hard drops on my face and then nothing, the sky clear to the east above the town, and I don't know why, but I thought, This is where I'd like to be when the first real snows blow in, turning everything white and still and silent—the sounds of those .22's behind me, and Roy's dog barking, and what must have been a whole pack of inchers popping, a signal from Paul to let me know he was there at the river like he said he'd be, waiting.

I sat down and let the knapsack slide from my shoulders, and I dangled my feet over the edge of the catwalk and held onto the guardrail, first with both hands, then with just one, and then slowly, I eased that hand away, too, and cupped them both around my mouth and shouted, "Here I am. Hey, up here." And then I yelled, "Phyllis Sellgrin, you have a beautiful bod and I love you. I LOVE YOU." And I yelled to my father, "Look, no hands," and I held them in front of my face, palms inward, and I thought, Hands, and I remembered the only thing I ever remembered about my mother, how she cooled me down with rubbing alcohol that time when I got very sick, that time right before she died. So I called to her, too: "Mother, where are you?" and I started to cry when the clouds covered the moon, and I leaned forward and looked straight down into all that dark and said to myself, "Shh, shh, that's enough," and I got out the beer and opened it and took a long swig, followed by a second, and a third, and put the bottle down half empty beside me.

I closed my eyes for what seemed a long time, and when I opened them the lights in most of the houses had gone out. But not in ours. I knew my father was asleep on the couch. I couldn't make him out, not even with the scope cranked up to the highest power, but I used our house as a point of reference to find Paul's, and I could see clearly two people in the kitchen kissing across the table. I could not make out the man. Maybe it was Paul's dad come back after all these years, but probably not. More likely it was a boyfriend passing through. Mrs. Burkholder was a very pretty woman. Even my father, who said some cruddy things sometimes about the Indians, said she was really something before all the booze, a true knockout.

I thought the man was going to touch her more than he did. But she was the one pulling him close, kissing him hard on the lips and for a long time before she let go of him and sat back in her chair. She didn't walk him out but he found the porch light and turned it on and then, after a couple minutes, the headlights, and I watched the car drive out of town, winding right past where Paul would be sitting alone, and I wanted at that moment for him to know that he was the best friend I ever had or ever would have and that we'd stick together no matter what, even if it meant going into the army.

"Paul, Paul Burkholder," I shouted, though I knew he could not hear me. "This one's no dud and it's for you, buddy," and I wedged the Roman candle into the wire mesh of the catwalk, the nose pointing upward, and I ignited the fuse and stood up and moved a few feet away. The rocket exploded into a red canopy of stars and, like a flare, lighted the whole tower, enough so I could see to climb onto the guardrail and stretch out my arms wide enough to hug this town we all claimed we hated, but didn't at all. And that's what I'd tell Paul, and Jimmy too. I'd say, "Listen up, you guys." I'd say, "Listen, there are people in this town who will always make us sad." And maybe we'd get talking about how we probably would stay here for a while, smoking their cigarettes and drinking their beer, which wasn't all that wrong. And anyway, it was fun some nights when we were together, we all had to admit that, getting tipsy and laughing to beat hell and keeping our lives in balance.

Bud and Goliath
in the Batting Cage

My dad and his older brother, Doyle, married the Husky twins in the same ceremony, which, four years later when we were born, made me and Flushy Lacrois double cousins. We were only four months apart in age, and we were in the same grade and, growing up, always best buddies. People sometimes said the resemblance was spooky and my father said spooky is right because he had a lot of gripes against his brother. He said *that* half of the family, meaning Doyle, not only laughed when he burped or farted, but made a sport out of it. No manners, he said, no modesty. He said, "There's your unmistakable difference."

But that wasn't all of it. The real difference was my mother's suicide when I was six and my father falling in love years later with Flushy's mom who was crazy and restless and who Flushy said had talked a lot about divorce, and I knew she had moved out at least a few times on Doyle, but never for very long. They were together again and had been for quite a while and, although they didn't seem like the happiest couple in the world, they seemed to me to be doing okay.

Recently they had bought, paying cash my father told me, a used motor home with low miles and red-and-blue stripes on all the trim and a decal of an Indian chief on each door. Doyle, all smiles, maneuvered it slowly backwards, using the sideview mirrors, into our driveway to show it off early one Sunday morning. He told us to sit in the swivel chairs in back, and then he turned on the air conditioner full blast, and then the staticky TV suspended from the ceiling, and then he poured himself half a glass of bourbon over ice, and me and my father split a bottle of Dr Pepper. After he left, my father turned to me and said that the thing must have been assembled in hell. It was pretty ugly all right, but Doyle loved it, having tested it out already on an overnighter to Tahquamenon Falls. Now he and my aunt were getting ready to crisscross the country, searching, Doyle said, for a better place to be for the rest of their lives. Which sounded kind of funny to me because he was the one always argued that the tribes should stay together, meaning the family. He said friends were friends, but they weren't blood. But he claimed he'd grown disenchanted with the U.P., living so long and so far up in the boonies, especially during the winters, ever since his knees had gotten worse. If he stayed, he said, he'd have to get new ones, plastic knees that wouldn't feel the cold. Uh-uh, he said, nope, he couldn't see the rewards in that. Easier in the long run to simply move out, he said. Unload the house and all the furniture and start over someplace else. My aunt wasn't so sure, but Doyle kept saying, someplace warm, maybe Texas, maybe stick a deposit on a condominium on the Gulf. He mentioned shrimp and redfish and a power boat for the ocean. He said it was a buyer's market down there. He said a guy with half a brain could ill afford to wait much longer.

Unlike my father, Doyle was in decent shape financially. He

boasted how the army had to issue him a check each month forever, meaning his lifetime, because of a freak accident he suffered when he was eighteen and stationed at Camp LeJeune. Add that, my father said, to his disability pay at the plant and you've got a double dipper, a guy with a lot of free time on his hands and a lot of walking-around money. I thought that was a joke, the walking-around part, given the way Doyle limped and sometimes had to use a cane, but my father didn't laugh when I did and I could see that he was angry. He rarely mentioned Flushy's mom by name, but he did right then. He said, "Ellen's loony if she lets him withdraw all their savings and do something dumb, lets him pull up stakes like that." He paused, and then he said, "There's nothing wrong with her legs," which was true, and which I know now is the kind of comment that can lead to trouble when it's said about another man's wife, even your own brother's wife. But I agreed. I said, "You've got that right," and he nodded at me a couple of times and walked away into the house.

So Flushy came to live with us that summer while they were gone, and they left him the Impala and a key to check the house now and then, and we both got jobs, for minimum wage, loading baseballs into the machines at the batting cages up on Route 10. My father, while cooking us breakfast and listening to us gripe one morning, told us about his first job, setting candle pins by hand at the Knights of Bohemia. Their hall was in Marquette where he and Doyle were born, he said, and there was a bowling alley in the basement, before lanes anywhere went automatic. And he said he'd broken the same finger twice, the little one on his right hand, and he showed us how it was still crooked, but he said, "Hey," and shrugged it off like no big deal. But I could tell he still held a grudge when he told us how the Knights would get drunk and, sometimes wearing those goofy hats and uniforms, wait for him to reach down from his platform suspended a couple of feet above the lane. Then they'd roll a ball as hard as they could. "Just an idiot stunt," he said, "booze will do it," and he told us how there was no ventilation and that it was hot and dark and that most of the time he could hardly breathe. He said, whenever he got hurt, he'd look upside down to where they were standing and laughing and yelling at him to get the goddamn pins on the red circles next time. They were foul-mouthed, he said. "Fucking kid," they'd call him, "fucking saphead." He was only twelve then, having lied to them about his age, and he said he never answered back and lied to his father about his fingers because he wanted to save up some money for a new bike and knew his father would make him quit, maybe go down there with him to straighten a few things out. But he said he did tell Doyle and the two of them, after midnight, sneaked out of the house and egged the windshields of a bunch of cars in the Knights' parking lot, including the Exalted Ruler's Cadillac, which filled the only reserved spot. Flushy had never heard this story, but I had and I hated the Knights, all of them, no matter what they were Knights of—Bohemia or Columbus or Pythesis. Horses' asses, I always called them, damn cruel bastards.

What we did wasn't dangerous, and the owner, Mr. Stefanyk, was a nice guy, though the job got old real fast, and sometimes I wished me and Flushy could stand side by side, our mitts on, catching and ducking line drives, five or six batters at a time spraying balls at us. Instead, we collected the balls in baskets when there were no customers, no out-of-shape hackers trying to show off for the girlfriend or the wife and kids, almost all of them tourists.

The part of the job I liked best was when my father stopped by late in the afternoon each Friday on his way home from work at the sheet metal plant, his sleeves rolled up, and he'd always bring his own bat, an old Harmon Killebrew model which he kept in the back of the pickup, and when he gripped the handle you could see the muscles tighten in his forearms. It was neat the way he stepped right into the batter's box and scuffed up the dirt with his boots and took only a couple of slow practice swings before dropping the quarters into the slot and pressing the red button for fastballs. Mr. Stefanyk told me once that they crossed the heart of the plate, letter high, at eighty miles an hour, not exactly big league speed, he said, but close, very close, and, because of the risk, he had to pay a high insurance premium, but I knew it was good business, that it drew the people in. You had to be eighteen to enter that batting cage. It was advertised up on the highway billboard as Goliath, the fastest throwing arm in the midwest, kind of like the World's Largest Pie or the Cross in the Woods, something to get all those summer travelers to detour a few miles from the fat yellow lines of their trip-tiks.

I never saw anybody get good wood on even a single ball in there, nobody except my father, who'd connect on almost every pitch, driving them deep and hard into the net. Other guys would always bail out quick, ducking away or even falling backwards to the ground on the first pitch. They'd chuckle scared and go to another cage or lean their bat back in the rack and say stuff like "Jesus H. Christ," or "No thank you, Sandy Koufax," as though the mechanical arm were human, as though, in there without a helmet and crouched over the plate, you could take the next pitch on your temple and end up brain dead. Candyasses, Flushy called them, but my father said no. He said it made good sense sometimes to play it safe. He said on vacation what you wanted was to get away and stay laid-back and not lose big. "I guess," Flushy said, and I just shrugged it off, like so what?

"Here's laid-back," Flushy said, cracking his third Strohs and tumbling backwards across the length of the couch.

"Hey," I said, "what's the deal, slow down on the brews." We weren't supposed to be using the house like this with his parents away, but we'd met two girls at the cages, sisters who were staying the month in a rental over on Turtle Lake with their folks. They said they were bored and came on to us like gangbusters, saying they had wheels but no place to go, so we'd given them this phone number and we were waiting for them to call, to give them directions how to get here. My father was working fill-in for some OT, and he wouldn't be home until at least 1:00 A.M. When the girls had walked away Flushy said to me, "My, my, my said the spider to the fly."

And he was still at it, talking big, saying this is how working guys should unwind for the weekend, getting buzzed and waiting for the broads to show. He said, "You get the one with the ponytail," and I said back, "No way, uh-uh, she's flat as a roof shingle. And mousy," I said, "and she won't bang."

Flushy was laughing and trying to balance the can of beer on his stomach. "Cousin," he said, "let me instruct you on some of the finer points of foreplay. She'll bang all right. She will if you find her touchspot."

"Touchspot?"

"Yeah," he said, clasping his hands behind his head. "Their weakness, Buddy boy, you know, scratch 'em where they itch, but you've got to find where that is and it's not that easy. You can't just go poking them every place when they walk in the door. You're not a goddamn doctor."

"It's their tits they like touched," I said, and Flushy said back, "Buddy, there's a lot of sex babble which comes cheap but very few secrets, and I happen to know about touchspots and mostly they're not where you'd guess. And anyway, you'll scare 'em like that, half shit-faced and grabbing like some sex maniac for their knockers. You've got to go slow, you've got to size 'em up, Buddy."

"I did size them up, which is why I want the other one, Barb, the one with the bare feet and painted toenails."

"Okay," he said, "right there, the bare feet, I ask you, what does it mean?" He was sitting up now, leaning toward me, like he was serious for a change.

"Means she kicked her shoes off; I don't know," I said, and Flushy corrected me. He said, "It means, Buddy, now listen up, that she's got a foot fetish and that her touchspot is probably on her instep and if she's sitting on the floor with her legs crossed like girls always do, and you're lucky enough to be next to her, shit, you're home free."

"What if the touchspot is the tits?" I asked him. "What then?"

He got up and walked to the refrigerator for another beer and from the kitchen he yelled back, "Question: is she or is she not braless?"

I heard him open the can and I looked at the thermometer outside the window. It was after five o'clock and still sweltering, still above ninety degrees and humid and I said to Flushy, "T-shirt braless. All nipples," I said, "like she's rubbed them herself or something so they stick out."

"Shit," Flushy said, walking back, the cold can pressed to his forehead. "What a frightening thought, to get off touching your own touchspot. Hell," he said, "they discover that and they won't need nobody, except to talk to, and that ain't us, Buddy, that sure the Christ ain't you and me."

But it was—we yakked away to each other through a six-pack and a half, Flushy drinking all but a couple, plus a shot of his dad's Jack Daniels, because those two sisters never called, and now, no lights on inside and the house darkening, we were quiet.

"I guess we been ditched," Flushy said, turning his face away from the window fan where he'd been kneeling and staring out at the street. The blades spun so fast, he said, you could see right through them like they weren't even there, but when he pushed his cigarette through the screen guard, a shower of sparks exploded back into the living room, right onto the area rug. I didn't even move to help stamp them out. I just eased myself a little further into the disappointment of the night, hoping only that it would cool down and that the neighbors wouldn't call again to complain that the Beach Boys were playing too loud on the hi-fi. Not a half hour before, I had taken the press off Flushy's tennis racquet and was strumming the cat gut, pretending I was Brian Wilson on guitar, and me and Flushy would touch our heads together as we leaned over the hand-held beer can of a microphone, belting out a few verses of "Barbara Ann":

Went to a dance, looking for romance,
Found Barbara Ann so I thought I'd take a chance,
Barbara Ann, Ba-Ba, Barbara A-A-Ann . . .

Perfect harmony, I'd thought, the way only family can do it, but Flushy was slurring his words now and we were tuning out on each other and what we said wasn't worth saying because it would have taken someone completely sober and articulate and so precise to explain to us right then how this ditched feeling would *not* be important much longer in our lives, that what we were suffering at sixteen was not love but curiosity, and that soon enough a woman would appear, and she'd unbutton her blouse for real and not because we sent goosebumps rippling across her flesh after discovering her touchspot. She'd do it because there came a time for everyone when that thing happened.

I wanted to wake Flushy and try and tell him that, to say no big deal with those two girls we hadn't even had a chance to fuss over and who we'd most likely never see again, but he was out cold on the floor beneath the ignorant whirr of the fan, so when the phone rang it was me who answered it and accepted the collect call from his mom. The operator said, "Go ahead, ma'am," and Ellen said, "Hi Flushy," and I said, "No, it's me, Buddy," and she paused a few seconds and then she started to cry. She said, "Your father wasn't home, I tried there," and I said I knew, that he was at work, and she said for me to get a pen and a piece of paper, so I switched on the lamp and said, "Just a sec," and then I said, "Okay," and she read me all her flight information and I jotted it down. Then she asked how Flushy was and I said good, and that he'd gotten the Alamo postcard. She didn't ask to talk to him though and she didn't ask where he was or how work at the batting cages was going. She just said there'd been a downpour in El Paso and that now the pavement was steaming outside the phone booth and that she could see the stars again. Then she said, "Tell your father, tell Bud Sr., to pick me up tomorrow."

"I will," I said.

"And tell him I saw Lady Bird Johnson in a supermarket; he'll get a kick out of that, and tell him I learned a little something about seafood delicacies. Imagine that," she said, "the ocean," and then she laughed and stopped suddenly and started to cry again. She said one evening last week the sky turned organdy above the Gulf, and she said she'd never in her whole life seen such huge azaleas, but that none of it mattered because it felt like doom to her down there. "Buddy," she said, "Buddy, are you still there?" and I said, "Yes, I'm here."

"What time is it in Michigan?" she asked and I said I didn't know, pretty late, maybe around midnight and she said the trip at the end had not gone well, that driving to Texas was a lot of nonsense, pure nonsense. She said, "Doyle and I don't belong down here, the people don't have anything in common with us." Then she paused and she said, "And I don't think Doyle and I belong together anymore either. That's why I'm flying home, Buddy, that's what I wanted to say, so I'm going to hang up now," and she did, without saying goodbye.

"I got it under control," I said to Flushy, "just get in the car," and I held the seat forward and he fell into the back. He'd made it to the bathroom, hugging the throne for a good half hour, first while throwing up, then for the dry heaves, and when I went back inside I flushed the toilet again, and then a third time after dumping in the cigarette butts from the ashtray. I locked the door on my way out and hid the empty beer cans in a grocery bag in the trunk. I didn't have a license but I drove anyway, hoping to get Flushy into bed before my father got home. But when I pulled up to the curb, there he was, sitting bare-chested on the steps of the front porch. I got this kind of sick feeling in my stomach, my hands clammy on the steering wheel, and I thought for a crazy couple seconds about driving away, I didn't know where to, but he did something strange—he stood slowly up and he waved to me, waved almost in slow motion, like he'd been waiting for me to arrive in a dream. I did not walk toward him until the arc of the sprinkler disappeared along the dark edge of the lawn, then I crossed. He was not angry when he said, "You're driving," and I nodded yes and he asked, "Beer too?" and I said, "A couple, earlier."

"And Flushy?" he asked, "he all right?"

"He's sick," I said, "he's passed-out in the back seat," and I turned sideways and pointed toward the car which seemed sort of ghostly white. But I could tell my father was staring beyond it, staring at the red lights blinking on top of the smokestack of the sheet metal plant where he'd worked for over twenty years and where, in winter, the snow was always real black on the sidewalks and on Union and Keefe avenues before the plows came through. Sometimes you could smell the burning from here, but not tonight, not with a breeze blowing now from out of the west. I thought he might say something about the alkies he worked with and about how drinking was a disease and how only dumb shits got started so young and then couldn't stop and ended up wrecking their lives. But he said none of that. I think he was listening to the music of the wind chimes and that he was unsure how to say what was going through his mind right then.

"Aunt Ellen called," I said, and he looked over at me and I could see, under the globe of the porch light, that his eyes were puffed and red as though he hadn't worn his goggles at work.

"Called who?"

"I answered," I said, "we were at Flushy's, so she talked to me. Twice she cried," I said. "She said she wants you to pick her up tomorrow at the airport in Marquette."

"What time?" he asked and I handed him the piece of paper from my pocket. He didn't have his glasses on, so he held the paper away from his face and toward the porch light. I told him what Ellen had said about her and Doyle not doing so good together and my father said, "There comes a time to be done with things; that marriage wasn't meant to last." He

paused then and I think he might have told me something I
didn't want to hear, something personal, if Flushy hadn't
gotten out of the car and slammed the door and leaned back
against it, his arms folded, like he was waiting for the verdict
about whether we were in big trouble or not. I signaled for
him to come on and he started slowly and a little wobbly
across the lawn. Then he stopped and looked up like it had
suddenly started to rain, and he held out his hands, and I
don't know, maybe he was still too drunk to see the stars or
the moon or to remember, when he started again toward the
porch, that my father, who'd walked back into the house, had
been standing there at all.

Flushy slid a pat of butter between his banana pancakes and,
with his butter knife, spread the Karo syrup until it dripped
over the sides. But he ate only a few bites and then he lowered
his head into his hands, the heel of his fork sticky on the
kitchen table.

"They never showed, right?"

"Wrong," I said, "they came by but you were so crocked I
had to ding them both, the old double-whammy, two hands
in the bush."

"Yeah," he said, and I could tell the joke was dead. "Your
father ticked?" he asked.

"He's not exactly thrilled," I said, but I thought that maybe
he was, about Ellen coming home alone, and Flushy said,
"Shit." He said, "Christ Almighty, it feels like somebody
dropkicked my head."

After I told him about the telephone call he went upstairs
and took a cold shower and a half hour later we were cruising
toward Lake Superior where, walking into the dunes earlier
that summer, we'd come across a woman sunbathing nude.
We stood above and behind her and we didn't move for a long
time. Her head was tilted toward us but she had sunglasses
on and we couldn't tell if her eyes were open or not. She
looked like the Bain de Soleil ad, minus the white swimsuit,
her dark hair pulled back from her forehead into a bun. I

remember, later, driving home, how Flushy had said, "Tell me it wasn't a mirage," and I said, watching the heat rise from the pavement in front of us on the highway, "Not from my angle she wasn't," and he said, "Nor from my angle either, the right angle in my pants."

But all the apparitions had evaporated on this trip and we didn't get out of the car. Flushy nosed it up to the guardrail at the edge of the bluffs and killed the engine and we both stared down at the charter boats trolling the dropoff for lakers. He almost never had the radio off, but it was off now and he opened a pack of Pall Malls and I took one and pushed in the lighter until it clicked and I held it for Flushy and then I lit my own. Flushy's bongos were on the seat between us, and I fitted them between my knees and started soft-tapping with my thumb and finger.

"It's weird shit," he said, "when your parents don't love each other much. I wish they'd just do it, get the goddamn divorce, 'course they won't."

"Maybe this time," I said.

"Nah," Flushy said, "they could give a clinic on how to fuck-up a marriage and still stay married. You'd figure they'd outgrow this shit, but they won't, they'll never get it right, neither one of them."

The dashboard clock said 11:40 and, if the plane was on time, I guessed my father would be carrying Ellen's suitcase right about now from the baggage claim. I imagined him, once outside, reaching over and squeezing her hand, and opening the door for her to the pickup and closing it and, before lifting the suitcase into the back, thinking, during that briefest hesitation at the tailgate, that in an hour or two or later that night, they'd be lovers.

"No way," Flushy said, as though I'd been thinking out loud, and I said, "No way what?" and he said, "No way am I ever getting hitched," and I said, "You'll outlive that statement by a couple of kids and a collie and a charcoal grill in the backyard."

"You don't expect me to respond to that," he said, and I

said back, "I do, I do, I do," and I did a kind of thumb roll on the tight hide of the bongos and he said, "Gimmie those," and he grabbed them and tossed them over his shoulder into the back seat. "My fucking head," he said, and flicked his cigarette out the window and closed his eyes and massaged the bridge of his nose like I'd seen my father do sometimes late at night, though never because of a hangover, and his fingers pressing harder than Flushy's, and higher up like he was trying to rub the deep creases out of his forehead. Flushy and my father did look alike—that same dark shiny hair and high cheekbones and long thick eyelashes—all Lacrois characteristics, inherited, my father boasted, from our French ancestors who'd immigrated north all the way from Paris, and then he'd smile and add, Paris, Michigan. He also used to joke about how, when he and Doyle started working together at the plant, you could always tell the Lacrois brothers by the silver metal shavings in their pant cuffs. Still shaking them out all these years later he'd say those were the dominant "jeans," and he'd spell the word so we'd get the pun, and he'd say, but hey, please, no factories for the new generation of Lacrois boys. "Be doctors," he'd tell me and Flushy, "so we'll have someone to take care of us in our old age." I always liked it when people told me I resembled my old man, that I'd gotten both his good looks and his good sense of humor.

Flushy looked like he was asleep, so I lowered the visor and blew smoke into the mirror and squinted so that my reflection blurred until I resembled someone else, maybe that sad ghost on my mother's side that continued to drift and drift through all of our lives. I used to pray that her suicide was not in my blood. "'Course it's not," Flushy tried to assure me once. "It's a recessive trait, a woman thing," and in our family that was true—Aunt Ellen's depressions seemed much worse than anybody else's. Flushy was always telling me how her moods changed so fast and how that wore Doyle down and how therapy was all a crock, a giant waste of time and money. And he took me into their bathroom once, locking the door behind us, and he opened the medicine cabinet and

showed me her prescriptions, bottles of light gray oblong
pills. He dropped one into his palm and he said, "Look, the
size of a .22 shell," and using his finger like a pistol barrel to
his temple, and cocking his thumb, he said, "Ka-bam," which
I didn't think was funny and I told him to shut his trap and
later he said he was sorry. All he'd said at breakfast this
morning about his mom was that she was scared to death of
flying, scared to death about what was waiting for her in the
next life. It's what kept her alive, he said, fear. Which wasn't
exactly the most chipper attitude in the world. But who
knows, maybe she believed, staying alive, that she could
finally get right what hadn't been right so far. Though I
didn't believe even then that people knew how to do that very
well, and that the new hope of change soon vanished into the
cruel future that reminded us, in every mirror and photograph and storefront window, that whatever loneliness we'd
ever carried and would carry again would always stay with
us, pointing and calling us by name.

Which is what my father did, meeting us late that afternoon
on the flagstone walkway, though he only said, "You and you,
follow me," and he motioned us away from the house toward
the garage and, after we entered, he closed the door. Then he
raised one foot on the blades of the snowblower and leaned
forward and said, "Come here, come over here close," and
we did, and he said, "You boys, well, listen to me," and he
seemed more intense when he paused than I'd ever seen him.
Then he cupped his hands on the back of our necks and pulled
our faces close to his, like he was about to kiss or threaten us
or, when his mouth finally opened, say something that would
come out so slowly and so quietly that I'd remember it only
as a dream. Neither Flushy nor I tried to pull away, and my
father did not speak, but in his eyes he did and all they said
was "trouble." Not what kind or how much but in that un-
blinking stare there was no mistaking one thing—Ellen was
staying in the house with him, and either she did not want to
see us yet or my father did not want her to. So when he let us

go and took out his wallet and handed us each a couple of bucks and told us go grab a sub at Paesano's, we did, and while we waited in the back booth for our order to come up, I watched, out the window, a woman in a Georgetown sweatshirt get out of a red Mustang and enter the side door and wait a few minutes at the counter for a pizza to go. Flushy's back was to her.

"Where's Georgetown?" I asked him.

"I don't know, in Jamaica, I think, a town in Jamaica, why?"

"Just thinking of women and exotic places to go away from here."

"Yeah," he said, "Georgetown might be good," and he got up to get our subs when our number was called, and I could see him watching the tan backs of that woman's legs as she left. She placed the pizza box on top of the trunk while she searched her pocketbook for her keys, then the back pockets of her cut-offs, patting her rump a couple of times with both hands and leaving them there while the guy with the floppy white chef's hat and apron walked toward her, dangling the keys. I liked the way she stood facing him and didn't move, her legs apart, and how she smiled that flirty kind of smile that said I'd forget my head if it weren't screwed on. I wished it had been me handing her the keys, maybe asking her name. I would have opened the car door for her and closed it and waited by the windbreak of poplars, watching her drive away. It had gotten real dark out and leaves shimmered, the frantic way poplars do before it storms.

"It's going to rain," Flushy said, sliding my sub across the table to me. And almost immediately it started to thunder and then much louder right above us and then it poured. Flushy ran outside to close the car windows and I pressed my face to the screen and I could smell the pavement cooling down and the temperature dropping fast and then I could see the first white clusters of hail, then the whole lot turning white with ice that smoked after it hit, and everyone staring out the windows and the kitchen help leaning against the

doorjamb under the entrance overhang and the power going
suddenly off and nobody saying a thing. I thought of Ellen
waking frightened from a nap and my father going to her and
sitting on the edge of the bed, stroking her long dark hair
back from her forehead. I imagined him leaning over to kiss
her and her, lips parted, kissing him back. I imagined her
under the sheet in a white slip and my father pulling the
sheet slowly back to her waist and her turning completely
over and closing her eyes for whatever he'd do next which I
forced myself not to imagine. Instead I thought of Flushy
alone in the front seat of the Impala and the windows and
windshield fogged and Doyle on the interstate, maybe somewhere in Nebraska, heading home, completing the scene.
Which I figured was close to the way things were at that
moment of the day in our lives. And I don't know why, but I
pictured the world then as black and white and silent, like
old home movies, even when the lights blinked on and Flushy
walked toward me, pulling his soaked T-shirt away from his
skin and shivering as he sat back down. He wiped his face
with a couple of napkins and said, "Huh, what?" but I hadn't
spoken so I just shook my head.

"I'm freezing my nads off," he said, and he lifted his sub
with both hands and kind of cocked his head, like maybe I
was going to snap a picture, and we ate then with my father's
money, and for a while neither one of us mentioned his name.

When Flushy finally did, he called him a backstabber. I had
turned the car radio to a big band station just for laughs, and
for maybe ten minutes we'd been listening to Glenn Miller
and the Ray Coniff singers, music my father and Doyle both
liked and played on holidays when we'd all get together.
Flushy finally said, "Come on, turn that shit off."

He wasn't drunk, but he'd had a few more of his father's
beers while we'd been driving in the country, killing time,
talking about quitting our jobs, about solutions to boredom
and about how boredom had limits and then you had to do
something or you'd be just another asshole contributing to
that inertia for the rest of your sorry life.

But the conversation had changed. Flushy said, "Yeah, that's right, a backstabber." Then he checked his rearview mirror like somebody was coming up on us around the wide curves of the marsh.

"Like Ellen's not part of it?" I said. "It's all my father's fault, is that it, am I right?"

"He's taking advantage of her," Flushy said. "She's confused, she's confusing my father and your father," and I stared down the V-beam of the headlights between the bogs and I thought of their faces superimposed, my dad's over Flushy's dad's, then changing, one to the other and back, sometimes smiling, sometimes angry the way I'd seen them both get, but never at each other. And I thought about how me and Flushy, even though we joked about it, both wanted that one girl named Barb and how, had she showed at the house that night, she would have had to choose between us because we were not the same. Or the same and different, which is what I believe men and women who are married or were once married are attracted to, the safety and the mystery deflected against each other.

"He hadda go do it, didn't he, he just hadda do this," Flushy said.

"Maybe they're in love," I said, "you ever think of that?" and Flushy said back, "What's that got to do with anything, Jesus Christ, how's that an excuse against what could happen to my father and to us and to the two of them too? How does all that get sorted out? Love, here's to that kind of love," and he grabbed another beer and opened it and chugged it and heaved the empty can whistling onto the road. He burped and breathing hard he said, "It must run on your side of the family cause you're a sleazebag too, you're a fucking sleaze, Buddy," and I don't know what he said after that because sometimes you have to stop listening to the tangle of too many words and take just certain ones inside your head and know that you heard those right and what they meant and those are the ones you act on. So I closed my fists and, when he glared over at me, still talking loud and mean, I hit him as hard as I could in the face and the car swerved sharply into the other lane but he didn't let go of the steering wheel and righted the car and when he touched the brakes and slowed way down, I leaned over and smacked him again and this time he turned one shoulder up and held his right hand under his nose to catch the blood.

And I knew, in the silence that followed, that what had happened would cost us, and I also knew if you had to wonder at what expense, which I did, then the damage would be considerable and permanent, and to speak, to say anything, would only devalue what the rage of those few minutes had been. So as Flushy drove I turned away and watched the bog mist rise and I listened to the intermittent croaking of frogs and, when he finally stopped in front of my house, I did not hesitate to get out of the car, and I did not lean back in to apologize because to square things between us then could not be done. And walking toward the house I did not care if I heard love moans or crying or soft talking from the kitchen, whatever adult love sounded like. And I did not care if I saw Ellen's underthings on the hassock or on the floor by the couch or hanging on a hook in the bathroom, or her compact on the vanity, or her bottle of shampoo on the edge of the bathtub. I only wanted to splash some cold water on my face and go to my bedroom and lie down. But before I turned the doorknob the porch light went on and, behind the beveled oval of glass, before I opened the door, I could see the outline of my father, a kind of shadow-man, standing in his white Jockey shorts.

"You home?" he asked when I stepped in, which may sound like a dumb question, but no question is dumb when its source is sadness, so I said, "Yes, I'm home," and I've since found that conversations of this kind go quickly if those first words do not indulge the weaknesses of guilt or blame.

"Sit down?" he said, and I nodded okay and stepped by him into the living room and I was glad that he did not turn on a lamp. What he described first was the sound of the propellers shutting down and how Ellen was the last one off the plane, how she waved down to him from the top stair and how, because of the airport construction, he listened to her high heels scud along the wooden planking as she ran toward him, opening her arms, embracing him. He mentioned her cashmere sweater and a short string of pearls. He described how she sat very close to him in the pickup and put her head on his shoulder and that it was not the first time he'd been with her like that, willingly, one time even leaving work midmorning, allowing what shouldn't happen in a small town to happen anyway, though until right now, nobody had found them out. He explained that Ellen's urgency to be with him always faded soon after they'd gone to bed, a few times in different motels and once at her house and now here. Whenever she needed him, he went to her. When she didn't, he stayed away, often for several months. And that was the trade-off: the permanent incompleteness for those brief hours of love.

"Is it worth it?" I asked him and he said, "Yes, I think so, mostly I think it is," and that did not surprise me. "And Doyle?" I asked, "What about him?"

"It's like he has blackouts, Buddy. Maybe it's the booze but he doesn't see things, essential things, and it's that blindness that has ruined his marriage, not this affair. Affairs are always elsewhere, and I don't mean in motel rooms, I don't mean that for God's sake. What I'm telling you is that affairs occur because a marriage has already collapsed," which I guessed was true a lot of the time, but I didn't care because I liked Doyle who I figured would arrive in a day or two with a bunch of fireworks, expecting that him and me and Flushy would blow them off some night after a barbecue in his backyard. And I felt bad that it most likely wouldn't happen and that nobody would tell him why.

"Enough?" my father asked, and I nodded yes, and then he said, "Let's go hit some balls," and I told him the cages closed at eleven, which of course he knew, and he said, "You've got the key?" and I said, "To get inside I do, but not to turn on the spots," and he said, "You drive," and he pulled on his pants and handed me the keys from his pocket and I went outside while he laced up his boots and it was then that I started to cry, the way you do sometimes and still manage to keep the tears inside your eyes. I stared up at the stars and swallowed and wiped my nose with the back of my hand. And I was okay a few minutes later when my father got in beside me and shut the door and let me drive without giving me any advice, without a single instruction.

I inched up as close as I could behind the batting cage, the white rubber plate centered directly between the high beams, and my father, staring straight ahead, said, "Pitchers should have simple names—Lefty or Doc or Whitey or Dutch, not Goliath. This isn't the Bible," he said. "This is baseball!"

But it wasn't, not really. It was a machine with a piston and a huge, tightly coiled spring, manufactured, I noticed once, in Peoria, Illinois. If the arm squeaked, we oiled it and it did not complain of stiffness or soreness and it could throw a million pitches without warming up, not at a catcher crouched and flashing signs, but at a padded wall painted to resemble a giant mitt. And there were no bleachers or dugouts or hot-dog venders, and nobody cheering or keeping score except for Mr. Stefanyk counting his profit at the end of each day.

My father had already taken his quarters from his plastic change purse and had unlocked the main gate and he was standing just outside the perimeter of the headlights, which I turned off after he stepped up to the plate and turned toward me and nodded. Then I listened as he connected, whack . . . whack . . . whack, pitch after pitch, his blind rhythmic swing. But I knew it really wasn't all that tough once you got your timing, and if you weren't afraid, which my father once told me some ballplayers were after seeing, close up, their first brushback pitch, legal in the big leagues but dangerous as hell, and that some guys who'd been beaned had died or ended their careers, wearing a metal plate in their skulls. One pitch, he'd said, and you could figure up your lifetime average. But I knew Goliath was going to keep firing strikes and that neither me nor my father would figure out much of anything, me staring into the darkness from the cab of the truck, and him imagining clutch base hits or two-baggers or the dramatic extra inning home run with each big swing. But I didn't believe there would be any heroic winning for him, nor for Ellen nor Doyle nor for Flushy and me, not this season when we'd already begun to count up the losses.

No, what he played wasn't baseball. And it wasn't the Bible either—at best a parody of it: Bud and Goliath in the Batting Cage. And I smiled thinking of that and how we believed sometimes that we could pull off the miraculous, slaying all those grotesque giants and ghosts of passion and loneliness who gathered during our lifetimes to haunt us.

Which I guess was what my father was doing with his bat in the dark cage, and Doyle when he left for Texas and had to drive back alone in his RV, and Ellen, who phoned long-distance and cried, trying to name after a storm the exotic images of grief. Which for me were not the ocean or organdy sky, but my mother's diaphanous face floating toward me almost every night in a dream. And Flushy, my double cousin and look-alike, who believed people should not marry, and that there are women in this world so vulnerable they would scream, undressing someday for him when he touched them. And me? I made no effort to defeat or confirm a thing. I just sat there and smoothed my sweaty hair back with both hands and breathed deeply, in and out, and I believed it was by that sound I most resembled our family, by that and the ordinary, unmistakable features of our hearts.